BUILDING YOUR
NEW TESTAMENT
GREEK VOCABULARY

Building Your New Testament Greek Vocabulary

Robert E. Van Voorst

WILLIAM B. EERDMANS PUBLISHING COMPANY
GRAND RAPIDS, MICHIGAN

Copyright © 1990 by Wm. B. Eerdmans Publishing Co.
255 Jefferson Ave. S.E., Grand Rapids, Mich. 49503

Printed in the United States of America

Library of Congress Cataloging-in-Publication Data

Van Voorst, Robert E.
    Building your New Testament Greek vocabulary / Robert E. Van Voorst.
        p.   cm.
    Includes bibliographical references and index.
    ISBN 0-8028-0486-1
    1. Greek language, Biblical—Vocabulary. 2. Bible. N.T.—Language,
    style.   I. Title.
PA863.V36   1990
487'.4—dc20   90-37068
                                                                CIP

To My Father and Mother
Robert and Donna Van Voorst

Ἐν ὅλῃ καρδίᾳ σου δόξασον τὸν πατέρα σου καὶ μητέρα·
τὶ ἀνταποδώσεις αὐτοῖς καθὼς αὐτοὶ σοί;

Contents

Preface

Learning a Greek vocabulary large enough for rapid reading of the New Testament is a daunting task. While a good knowledge of Greek grammar can be gained in a year of study, New Testament vocabulary typically demands much longer attention. This book seeks to aid in this task by enabling the student to build a vocabulary of New Testament Greek by using the principles of word formation and by drawing on the cognate relationships of most New Testament Greek words.

For more than two generations the best tool for learning the Greek vocabulary of the New Testament has been Bruce M. Metzger's *Lexical Aids for Students of New Testament Greek*.[1] This helpful book has been the standard in its field, and rightly so. Still, *Lexical Aids* has shortcomings. Using its lists of 1067 words organized by frequency in the New Testament, the student sees no cognate relationships between words; most memorization is rote.[2] Metzger does also list 690 words, many in addition to those in the frequency lists, by cognate. But because this cognate list does not include even half the words that are in the frequency list, it is unsuitable for comprehensive vocabulary learning. Moreover,

---

1. First edition, 1946; new edition, 1969. Princeton: published by the author.
2. Computer software programs for learning biblical Greek vocabulary are also based on frequency.

my practice and that of other teachers using *Lexical Aids* has been to assign the frequency lists with some thoroughness, but the cognate list only occasionally. Hence the need for one format combining frequency and cognate, a format that can enable the student to memorize Greek vocabulary as easily as possible and in a pedagogically sound manner.

Building Your New Testament Greek Vocabulary is organized as follows: Part One is a guide to using this book, and is directed especially to the student. Part Two is an outline of the basic principles of word building. It should be studied with some care before the student proceeds to the cognate lists in Part Three, as a knowledge of the rudiments of word building will make memorizing vocabulary easier and more effective.

Each word that appears five or more times in the New Testament appears once in Part Three or Part Four, in Part Three if it has any cognate(s) that also appear five or more times in the New Testament, in Part Four if it does not. The words in Part Three are arranged by cognate families in six sections according to the frequency of the most recurrent word in each family. Each word is given a basic English definition based on New Testament usage, and its frequency in the New Testament is listed. Occasionally a well-known English derivative is given to aid in memorization.[3] The lists in Part Four of those Greek words appearing five or more times in the New Testament without common cognates are also divided into six frequency groups. As in Part Three, basic English definitions and occasional English derivatives are given and the frequency of each word is listed.

The two sections listing words occurring five to nine times (III. G. and IV. G.) can be left aside by those who want to omit learning words of such low frequency that do not have more common cognates. Also, the frequency of each word in the cognate lists (Part Three) is noted, so that the teacher can assign for study any given frequency of Greek words.

---

3. Metzger also includes a good number of English derivatives in his lists. However, many of these words are unfamiliar to most students, even though they are words that students of Bible and theology should learn (e.g., "hamartiology," "macarism," "thaumaturge"). This use of unfamiliar words violates the pedagogical principle that the unfamiliar (here Greek words) should be learned via the familiar (their English derivatives). I have endeavored to restrict the derivatives to more familiar words.

The student should alternate between the corresponding sections of Parts Three and Four until both parts have been completed. As an aid to learning, each frequency section is divided into groups of about 20 to 30 words, which seems to be a good number to learn at one sitting.

Part Five lists the principal parts of selected important verbs, and Part Six lists ordinal and cardinal numbers. All of these verbs and numbers appear in Parts Three and Four, but are presented together again for the benefit of the student.

I have drawn the definitions in Parts Three and Four from the second edition of *A Greek-English Lexicon of the New Testament and Other Early Christian Literature* (hereafter BAGD), keeping closely to the New Testament usage.[4] For counting frequency I have used the *Concordance to the Novum Testamentum Graece*.[5] This concordance is based on the twenty-sixth edition of the Nestle-Aland *Novum Testamentum Graece*,[6] the text (but not the textual apparatus) of which is identical to that of the third edition of the United Bible Societies' *Greek New Testament*.[7] In determining cognate relationships, I have used as final authorities E. Boisacq's *Dictionnaire étymologique de la langue grecque*[8] and H. Frisk's *Griechisches etymologisches Wörterbuch*.[9]

I should like to thank here those who helped this project along in various ways. Professor George Landes of Union Theological Seminary (New York) encouraged and advised me as I began this book; it is patterned somewhat upon his *Student's Vocabulary of Biblical Hebrew Listed according to Frequency and Cognate*.[10] My colleagues in the religion department of Lycoming College, Eduardo Guerra and Richard Hughes, encouraged me to carry out this project in my first year of college

---

4. By W. Bauer; translated and revised by W. F. Arndt, F. W. Gingrich, and F. W. Danker. Chicago: University of Chicago Press, 1979. Copyright © 1957, 1979 by the University of Chicago. All rights reserved. Used by permission.
5. Third edition. Berlin: DeGruyter, 1987.
6. Stuttgart: Deutsche Bibelstiftung, 1979.
7. Stuttgart: United Bible Societies, 1983.
8. Heidelberg: Winter / Paris: Klincksieck, 1938.
9. Heidelberg: Winter, 1960.
10. New York: Scribners, 1961; now published by Macmillan.

teaching. Sheran Swank, the secretary for the department, did a most skillful job of putting the challenging manuscript on disk. My student assistant, Jeremy Owens, compiled the index and helped in reading the proofs. The Wm. B. Eerdmans Publishing Company was kind to take this book on, and its editor, John W. Simpson, Jr., made many helpful suggestions. While all these friends made this a better book, any errors that remain are mine alone. I have taken painstaking care in compiling the lists, but in a work like this errors are bound to creep in, and I would be grateful if these were communicated to me. Finally, my thanks are owed to my wife Mary and our two sons, Richard and Nicholas, for encouraging and assisting me in all my scholarly endeavors.

The quotation in the dedication is excerpted from Sirach 7:27-28: "With all your heart honor your father and mother; what can you give back to them that equals what they have given to you?"

> Robert E. Van Voorst
> Department of Religion
> Lycoming College
> Williamsport, PA 17701

Part One

Guide to Using This Book

In a year's course of studying Greek grammar students learn at most several hundred Greek words, usually as a part of each lesson in their textbook. But when they come to read the New Testament they find that this vocabulary is woefully inadequate for reading it with any speed or confidence. Often they spend more time looking up unknown words in the lexicon than directly reading the text itself, and they soon get discouraged. At this point in studying Greek several hundred other words should be learned, and the more the better.

Building Your New Testament Greek Vocabulary is designed to help the student of New Testament Greek cross that gap by learning all the words that occur five or more times in the New Testament. Such a vocabulary of New Testament Greek is sufficient for rapid, confident reading of the text. Part One is directed especially to the student as a brief guide to using this book to the fullest advantage in building a large vocabulary of Greek.

This book combines the *frequency* method of listing vocabulary (based on the number of times a word occurs in the New Testament) with the *cognate* method (based on word families). Cognates are understood here to be words that are related to each other by their possession of a common element, usually called a stem or root, and that are therefore related in meaning as well. Words that are cognate make up a word

1

family. To take an example from English, the words "believe," "belief," "unbelief," "believable," "believer," etc., are all obviously cognates. They share the root "believ-," and make up a family of words. Words in any language do not grow willy-nilly; they are formed in certain regular patterns, and to know the patterns employed in Greek word building is greatly to simplify the tedious process of memorizing New Testament vocabulary. Therefore, the student should carefully study Part Two, "Basic Principles of Greek Word Building," before proceeding to the word lists.

Each cognate group is organized as follows: Each entry in the group has a Greek word, its English definition, an English derivative where helpful, and a frequency number. The English definition is very basic, and is not at all intended to be comprehensive; for full definitions and nuance, BAGD should be consulted. Where an English derivative is given, it can be used as an aid to memorizing the particular Greek word from which it comes, but can also sometimes be used to remember other words in the cognate group as well. Finally, the frequency number can be noted but need not be remembered. Each cognate group begins with the most frequent word, which is in bold type. The group generally proceeds from there in alphabetical order, but not in a strictly uniform way, because very similar words are kept together for ease in memorization regardless of their alphabetical order.

The frequency lists in Part Four have the same basic entries as the frequency and cognate lists in Part Three: the Greek word, its definition, a derivative where helpful, and the frequency number. The Greek words in this list are not necessarily without any cognates in the New Testament, but those cognates that occur do so less than five times. The frequency lists in Part Four are organized according to the same rates of frequency as the lists in Part Three, and the student should alternate between the corresponding sections of Parts Three and Four.

The New Testament contains 1630 words that occur five or more times, all of which are listed here. (This does not include nouns that are always proper, since they are easily discernible from their Greek form.) Of these 1630 words, about 76% can be placed with cognates also occurring five or more times. If the student omits parts III. G. and IV. G., which list most of the words occurring 5-9 times (those that have not been grouped with more frequent cognates), the percentage of words remaining listed with cognates rises to 84%. That the great majority of New Testament Greek vocabulary can thus be listed and learned together with cognates more than compensates for the disadvantage of having to consult two sets of lists.

Although each student must find a system for learning vocabulary that works well for her or him, these suggestions may be helpful:

(1) Begin by studying the words in this book as they are listed in their word families. Note their relationships to each other as far as these are evident. Use the margins of the pages to make notes about the words studied.

(2) When learning Greek words, repeat the word aloud several times. Pronouncing and hearing the words will help in memorizing them. Take care to accent the right syllable, and when repeating words keep the accent on this syllable. Not doing so complicates the task.

(3) In addition to saying the words aloud, write them out several times. Write and pronounce them together. The more ways that words are impressed on the memory, the more complete memorization will be.

(4) Note the English derivatives when they are given. The meaning of the English word will be suggestive of the meaning of the Greek word. Learn the Greek word by way of the actual English derivative *before* resorting to other, nonsensical associations with English words.

(5) Some students find flash cards helpful. While commercially-printed cards are available, it is best to write out one's own. Keep them in cognate groups, especially at first. Then they can be rearranged as one goes along so that more attention is devoted to new and difficult words.

(6) Words that stubbornly resist memorization—which happens to almost every student, and for no easily discernible reason—can often be learned by memorizing a short, familiar phrase from the New Testament in which these words occur.

(7) Using one's actual knowledge of Greek words and the principles of word formation, the student can often make an intelligent preliminary guess about the meaning of unfamiliar words, especially the

3

words of very low frequency not presented in this book. Such guesses should, of course, be soon checked against the lexicon.

(8) Constant review is essential to work Greek vocabulary from short-term memory into long-term memory.

Part Two

Basic Principles of Greek Word Building

The Greek language builds words in rather regular patterns. To know these patterns is to lighten greatly the chore of memorizing vocabulary, especially when memorizing cognate words. We will consider here only the most basic principles of word formation necessary for learning vocabulary. Those who desire more detail should consult a standard Greek grammar.[1] The two most frequent methods of building words are derivation and composition.

---

1. For example, H. W. Smyth, *Greek Grammar* (revised edition; Cambridge, MA: Harvard University Press, 1956), pp. 225-254; or F. Blass and A. Debrunner, *A Greek Grammar of the New Testament and Other Early Christian Literature,* ed. R. W. Funk (Chicago: University of Chicago Press, 1961), pp. 58-68. It is interesting to note that Blass-Debrunner-Funk's *Greek Grammar* can give a full discussion of word formation without any discussion of roots. The best treatment, and the one relied on here, is by J. H. Moulton and W. F. Howard, *A Grammar of New Testament Greek,* vol. 2, *Accidence and Word Formation* (Edinburgh: Clark, 1928), pp. 267-410.

WORD BUILDING BY DERIVATION

In derivation suffixes are added to a word stem to form different cognate words. For example, to the stem βασιλ-, which carries the notion of "rule, kingship," is added the nominal suffix -ευς to make βασιλεύς, "king"; the verbal suffix -ευω to make βασιλεύω, "I rule, am king"; and the adjectival suffix -ικος to make βασιλικός, "royal." In the course of this adding of suffixes the final part of the stem often undergoes various changes. The rules that govern these changes will not be discussed here, because students who have had some Greek grammar are already familiar with many of these changes as they appear in other contexts, and at any rate the stem is almost always recognizable.

The charts that follow give the *typical* significance of the most important suffixes used in building the vocabulary of the Greek New Testament. Some uses of suffixes will vary from this typical significance, but most adhere to it. The left-hand column lists the suffixes; suffixes for adjectives are in the nominative case and the masculine gender only, for reasons of space. The middle column gives the typical significance of each suffix. The right-hand column gives well-known words from the New Testament as examples of how particular suffixes join stems to build cognate words.[2]

---

2. Although we speak of "building" words from the "stem," note that these stems (which some grammarians call "roots") probably never had any existence apart from the words in their families. Stems or roots are *abstractions* from existing words, made for linguistic purposes. What T. O. Lambdin says about Hebrew roots is applicable to the Greek language: "The root is a grammatical abstraction from [cognate] words and not vice-versa; that is, because a root has no existence apart from its incorporation into words, it leads to a misunderstanding of the nature of language to say that words are derived from the root" (*Introduction to Biblical Hebrew* [New York: Scribners, 1971], p. 18). If this is recognized, the notion of stems/roots can be used as a valid grammatical construct in studying word formation and learning the vocabulary of the Greek New Testament.

6

A. Nominal Suffixes

Suffix	Typical Significance	Example from the New Testament
-ος	person, thing	θεός god, God
-της -τηρ -ευς	person, agent	κριτής judge (cf. κρίνω, I judge) σωτήρ savior (cf. σώζω, I save) βασιλεύς king (cf. βασιλεύω, I am king)
-τις -σις -ια	activity	πίστις faith (cf. πιστεύω, I believe) κρίσις judging (cf. κρίνω) οἰκονομία management, task (cf. οἰκονομέω, I manage)
-μα	result of an activity	γράμμα letter (cf. γράφω, I write)
-ια -σια -συνη -εια -οτης	abstraction, quality	σωτηρία salvation (cf. σώζω) ἐκκλησία church (cf. ἐκκαλέω, I call out) δικαιοσύνη righteousness (cf. δικαιόω, I justify) βασιλεία kingdom, rule (cf. βασιλεύω) νεότης youth, young age (cf. νεανίας, young man)
-ιον -ιδιον -ισκος	diminution	παιδίον infant (cf. παῖς, child) βιβλαρίδιον little book (cf. βίβλος, book) νεανίσκος young man, boy (cf. νεανίας)

7

B. Adjectival Suffixes

Suffix	Typical Significance	Example from the New Testament
-ιος	possession	*τίμιος* honorable (cf. *τιμή*, honor)
-ικος	belonging to	*πνευματικός* spiritual (cf. *πνεῦμα*, spirit)
-ινος	material, type	*σάρκινος* made of flesh, fleshly (cf. *σάρξ*, flesh)
-εος		*χρύσεος* golden (cf. *χρυσίον*, gold)
-ος	no definite meaning	*καλός* good, beautiful
-λος	beyond a general	*τυφλός* blind
-(α)νος	quality or attribute	*γυμνός* naked
-ρος		*νεκρός* dead

C. Adverbial Suffixes

Suffix	Typical Significance	Example from the New Testament
-ως (by far the most common)	manner	*δικαίως* justly, righteously (cf. *δίκαιος*, just)
-θεν	from where	*ἐκεῖθεν* from there (cf. *ἐκεῖ*, there)
-ιστί	in what language	*Ἑλληνιστί* in Greek

D. Verbal Suffixes

Suffix	Typical Significance	Example from the New Testament
-ω	state or action	ἄγω I lead
-έω		ποιέω I make, do
-άω		τιμάω I honor
-μι		παρίστημι I am present
-άζω	action	κράζω I cry out
-ίζω		βαπτίζω I baptize
-εύω		δουλεύω I serve (as a slave)
-όω	causation	δουλόω I enslave
-ύνω		αἰσχύνω I make ashamed
-αίνω		λευκαίνω I make white

WORD BUILDING BY COMPOSITION

A compound word is formed by the joining of two or more words. English does not form compounds as readily as did Hellenistic Greek, in which word formation through composition was very common.

The great majority of compound words in the New Testament are compound verbs. Compound verbs have a preposition as their first member and a verb as the second member. The precise nuance that the preposition adds to the verb varies, because the meaning of the preposition is often modified by the verb it joins. In addition to a local force (showing direction), several prepositions also sometimes strengthen or perfect the force of verbs with which they are compounded. English has a few examples of this: "eat" is strengthened in "eat up," "swallow" in "swallow down," etc. The student should be aware, though, that by Hellenistic times some of these perfectives had lost the force they originally may have had. Failure to recognize this when it occurs leads to "overtranslating" the verb. For example, one of the meanings of φιλέω is "I kiss," but the compound verb καταφιλέω does not signify an especially intense kiss. Here (as always) usage is determinative, for which a good lexicon should be consulted. The prepositions most often used as perfectives are: συν-, κατα-, ἀνα-, δια-, παρα-, and ἐκ-. They are translated in the chart below with "thoroughly."

A. Compound Verbs with Prepositional Prefixes

Prefix	Typical Significance	Example(s) from the New Testament
ἀνα- (ἀν-)	up, again; thoroughly	ἀναβαίνω I go up, embark ἀναζητέω I search after
ἀντι- (ἀντ-, ἀνθ-)	against, instead of	ἀντιλέγω I object to, oppose
ἀπο- (ἀπ-, ἀφ-)	away from; thoroughly	ἀποστέλλω I send away ἀπόλλυμι I destroy
δια- (δι-)	through, between	διέρχομαι I go through
εἰσ-	into, in	εἰσάγω I lead into
ἐκ- (ἐξ-)	out of, from; thoroughly	ἐξέρχομαι I go out ἐκζητέω I search out
ἐν- (ἐγ-, ἐμ-)	in, into	ἔνειμι I am in, am inside
ἐπι- (ἐπ-, ἐφ-)	on, upon	ἐπικαλέω I call upon
κατα- (κατ-, καθ-)	down, against; thoroughly	καταβαίνω I go down, disembark κατεσθίω I eat up, devour

10

μετα- (μετ-, μεθ-)	with, after	μετανοέω I repent (implies change)
παρα- (παρ-)	beside, near	πάρειμι I am near
περι-	round, about	περιτέμνω I circumcise (literally "cut around")
προ-	before (of time or place)	προέρχομαι I go before
προσ-	to; nearby	προσάγω I bring to; I come near
συν- (συγ-, συλ-, συμ-)	with, together; thoroughly	συνάγω I gather together συλλαμβάνω I seize, catch
ὑπερ-	over, above	ὑπεροράω I overlook, neglect
ὑπο-	under	ὑποτάσσω I put under, subject

The meaning that prepositional prefixes contribute to verbs can be illustrated by the many compounds in the New Testament of βάλλω, "I put, place, throw." ἀποβάλλω means "I throw off." ἐκβάλλω is "I throw out," hence "I expel." ἐπιβάλλω means "I lay upon." καταβάλλω means "I throw down," in the middle voice "I found, lay," especially used of laying a foundation. "I put around, clothe" is περιβάλλω. προβάλλω is "I put forward, put out." The meaning of συμβάλλω is not readily apparent; it is "I converse, consider, meet." The parts of this compound are hinted at by BAGD, which suggests that συμ + βαλλω is paralleled by our modern colloquial expression, "get it all together." Finally, ὑπερβάλλω is "I go beyond, surpass, outdo."

11

B. Compounds with Adverbial Prefixes

Compound words of all types can be formed by prefixing an adverbial particle or an independent adverb to a word or stem. The chief adverbial prefixes used in forming compounds in the New Testament are:

Prefix	Typical Significance	Example(s) from the New Testament
ἀ- (ἀν-) (by far the most common)	not, un-, dis-	ἄδικος unjust ἀπιστέω I disbelieve, am unfaithful
εὐ-	well, good	εὐαγγέλιον good news, gospel εὐεργετέω I do good
δυσ-	hard, un-, mis-	δυσεντέριον dysentery

C. Compound Nouns and Adjectives

Compound nouns and adjectives are also formed by joining two words, one of which is usually a noun. As in word building by derivation, changes often occur in the words joined. In compound nouns and adjectives this change almost always occurs at or near the point of conjunction. Fortunately for the student of Greek vocabulary, the two members of the compound are usually recognizable despite these changes, and we will not look directly at the separate members here. But for understanding compounds of all sorts, each member of the compound must be understood and taken into account.[3]

The two members of compound nouns and adjectives can be

---

3. In the word lists, compound verbs are listed by the second element, the verb. All other compounds are generally listed by the first element.

viewed as standing in various case relationships with each other. Most obvious is an accusative case relationship, where one member of the compound receives the action of the other as its "direct object":

νομοδιδάσκαλος teacher of the law
παντοκράτωρ ruler of all, hence "the Almighty"
οἰκοδεσπότης ruler of a house
ἀρχισυνάγωγος ruler of a synagogue

A dative case relationship may also be apparent:

εἰδωλόθυτος sacrificed to idols
θεοδίδακτος taught by God

Many compounds show a nominative case relationship. That is, the members of the compound stand in a predicate relationship, with the first usually describing the second:

μονογενής unique, only, one-of-a-kind
ἀρχιερεύς chief priest, high priest
ψευδοπροφήτης false prophet

CONCLUSION

To sum up this treatment of word building, perhaps it would be helpful to offer a rather comprehensive example of word building by both derivation and composition from one root. The root we shall employ is δικ, which in its word family signifies "right, just." Note how this stem joins the prefixes and suffixes listed above to form a whole family of words. (Not all word families are as full and well-formed as this, but this one is highly illustrative of the process.) Nouns formed by derivation and composition are:

δίκη punishment, justice
δικαστής judge

13

δικαιοσύνη   justice, righteousness
δικαίωμα   righteous deed
δικαίωσις   justification, acquittal
ἀδικία   unrighteousness
ἀδίκημα   sin, crime
ἐκδίκησις   retribution, punishment
δικαιοκρισία   righteous judgment

Adjectives formed from this root greatly resemble the nouns:

δίκαιος   just, righteous
ἄδικος   unjust, unrighteous
ὑπόδικος   responsible to, answerable to

The verbs of this word family are:

δικαιόω   I justify, pronounce righteous
ἀδικέω   I wrong, do harm
ἐκδικέω   I avenge, punish
καταδικάζω   I condemn

Finally, the adverbs are:

δικαίως   justly, righteously
ἀδίκως   unjustly, unrighteously

Part Three

New Testament Greek Vocabulary Listed by Frequency and Cognate

III. A. FAMILIES WITH ONE OR MORE WORDS OCCURRING 400 OR MORE TIMES

1. ἀκούω	I hear	(*acou*stic)	430
ἀκοή, -ῆς, ἡ	hearing, ear, report		24
εἰσακούω	I listen to		5
ὑπακούω	I obey		21
ὑπακοή, -ῆς, ἡ	obedience		15

ἀλλά	but, rather, yet		638
ἄλλος, -η, -ο	another, other	(*al*ien)	155
ἀλλήλων	each other, one another		100
ἀλλότριος, -ία, -ον	belonging to another, strange		14
ἀλλάσσω	I change		6
καταλλάσσω	I reconcile		6

ἄνθρωπος, -ου, ὁ	human being, person	(*anthrop*ology)	551
ἀνθρώπινος, -η, -ον	human		7

αὐτός, -ή, -ό	he, she, it; himself, herself, itself; even, very; same	(*auto*mobile)	5601
ἑαυτοῦ, -ῆς, -οῦ	himself, herself, itself		321
ἐξαυτῆς	at once, immediately		6

γίνομαι	I am, become, happen		670
παραγίνομαι	I come, am present		37
γεννάω	I beget		97
γενεά, -ᾶς, ἡ	family, generation	(*genea*logy)	43
γένεσις, -έως, ἡ	beginning	(*genesis*)	5
γένος, -ους, τό	race, stock	(*genus*)	21
γονεῖς, -έων, οἱ	parents		20
μονογενής, -ές	only, unique		9
συγγενής, -ές	related, akin to		9

2. δίδωμι	I give		415
δῶρον, -ου, τό	gift		19
δωρεά, -ᾶς, ἡ	gift, bounty		11
δωρεάν	freely		9
ἀποδίδωμι	I give away, give up; I render		48
μεταδίδωμι	I impart, share		5
παραδίδωμι	I hand over, hand down, entrust		119
παράδοσις, -εως, ἡ	handing over, tradition		13

ἐγώ[1]	I	(*ego*)	2666
ἐμός, -ή, -όν	my, mine		76
ἐμαυτοῦ, -ῆς	myself		37
ἡμέτερος, -α, -ον	our		8

εἰ	if		507
ἐάν	if		351

εἰμί	I am	(cf. *am*)	2461
ἄπειμι	I am absent		7
πάρειμι	I am present		24
παρουσία, -ας, ἡ	presence, coming	(*parousia*)	24
ἐξουσία, -ας, ἡ	power, authority		102
ἔξεστι	it is permitted, possible		32
ὄντως	really, certainly, in truth		10
ἔνι	there is		6

---

3. εἰς	into, in		1768
ἔσω	in, inside		9
ἔσωθεν	inside, within		12

ἐκ, before vowels ἐξ	from, out of	(e*x*hale)	916
εκτός	outside		8
ἔξω	outside, out		63
ἔξωθεν	from the outside, outside		13

---

1. The inflected forms of ἐγώ—ἐμοῦ, ἐμοί, etc.—are more clearly cognate to the rest of the words in this group than is ἐγώ.

ἔρχομαι	I come, go	636
ἀπέρχομαι	I go away	118
διέρχομαι	I go through	43
εἰσέρχομαι	I enter	194
ἐξέρχομαι	I go out, come out	218
ἐπέρχομαι	I come, come upon	9
κατέρχομαι	I come down	16
παρέρχομαι	I go by, (pass.) I pass away	30
προέρχομαι	I go forward, go before	9
προσέρχομαι	I go to, approach	86

4. **ἔχω**	I have, hold	711
ἀνέχομαι	I endure	15
ἀπέχω	I receive; I am distant; I abstain	19
ἐξῆς	on the next day	5
ἐπέχω	I hold fast; I aim at	5
κατέχω	I hold back, hold fast	18
μετέχω	I share, participate in	8
μέτοχος, -ον	sharing in	6
παρέχω	I give, cause	16
προσέχω	I pay attention	24
ὑπερέχω	I surpass	5

ἵνα	in order that, that	663
ἱνατί	why?	6

καί	and, also, likewise	9012
κἀγώ	and I, but I	84
καίπερ	although	5
κἀκεῖ	and there	10

κακεῖθεν	and from there		10
κακεῖνος, -η, -ο	and that one, and he		22
κἄν	and if, even if, if only		17

κατά	(with gen.) down, against; (with acc.) according to, along		476
κάτω	below, downward		9

κύριος, -ου, ὁ	master, lord, the Lord		719
κυριεύω	I am lord, I lord it over		7

5.

λέγω	I say, tell	(*legen*d)	2365
λόγος, -ου, ὁ	word, Word	(theo*logy*)	330
λογίζομαι	I reckon, think		41
ἀπολογέομαι	I defend myself		10
ἀπολογία, -ας, ἡ	defense, reply	(*apolog*etics)	8
διαλέγομαι	I discuss, speak	(*dialogue*)	13
διάλεκτος, -ου, ἡ	language	(*dialect*)	6
διαλογίζομαι	I consider, reason		16
διαλογισμός, -οῦ, ὁ	thought, doubt, dispute		14
ἐκλέγομαι	I choose, select		22
ἐκλεκτός, -ή, -όν	chosen, select	(*eclec*tic)	22
ἐκλογή, -ῆς, ἡ	election		7
εὐλογέω	I bless		42
εὐλογητός, -ή, -όν	blessed, praised		8
εὐλογία, -ας, ἡ	praise, blessing	(*eulogy*)	16
ὁμολογέω	I confess		26

19

ὁμολογία, -ας, ἡ	confession	6
ἐξομολογέομαι	I confess	10
προλέγω	I tell beforehand	15
συλλέγω	I collect	8

μή	not	1043
μηδέ	and not, but not	56
μηδείς, -δεμία, -δέν	no one, nothing	89
μηκέτι	no longer	22
μήποτε	that not, lest	25
μήτε	and not, neither, nor	34
μήτι	(a usually untranslated particle in questions that expect a negative answer)	18

6. **μετά**	(with gen.) with; (with acc.) after, behind	473
μεταξύ	between	9

ὁ, ἡ, τό	the	19904
ὅδε, ἥδε, τόδε	this	10
ὧδε	here	61

ὁράω	I see	449
ὅραμα, -ατος, τό	(a supernatural) vision	12
ἀόρατος, -ον	unseen, invisible	5

ὅς, ἥ, ὅ	who, which, what	1365
οἷος, -α, -ον	of what sort, such as	15
ὅσος, -η, -ον	as great, how great; as far, how far	110
ὅστις, ἥτις, ὅ τι	who, whoever	148
ὅτε	when	103
ὅτι	that, because, since	1297
οὗ	where, whither	54
ὅθεν	from where	15

οὐ, οὐκ, οὐχ	no, not	1630
οὐδέ	and not, nor; neither, nor	144
οὐδείς, -εμία, -έν	no one, nothing	227
οὐδέποτε	never	16
οὐκέτι	no more, no longer	47
οὔπω	not yet	26
οὔτε	neither, nor	87
οὐχί	not	53
ἐξουθενέω	I despise, reject	11

---

7. **οὗτος, αὕτη, τοῦτο**	this		1391
οὕτως	in this manner, thus, so		208

πᾶς, πᾶσα, πᾶν	all, every	(*pan*orama)	1244
ἅπας, -ασα, -αν	all, every		34
πανταχοῦ	everywhere		7
πάντως	certainly		8
παντοκράτωρ, -ου, ἡ	the Almighty		10

πατήρ, πατρός, ὁ	father	(*patr*istics)	414
πατρίς, -ίδος, ἡ	fatherland, hometown	(*patri*ot)	8

ποιέω	I do, make		568
περιποίησις, -εως, ἡ	preserving, possessing		5
ποιητής, -οῦ, ὁ	doer, maker	(*poet*)	6
χειροποίητος, -ον	made by human hands		6
ζῳοποιέω	I make alive		11

πολύς, πολλή, πολύ	much, many	(*poly*unsaturated)	418
πολλάκις	many times, often		18

πρός	(with dat.) near, at; (with acc.) to, toward		699
ἔμπροσθεν	(adverb) in front, ahead; (prep., with gen.) in front of, before		48

σύ	you		1066
σεαυτοῦ	yourself		43
σός, σή, σόν	your, yours		27
ὑμέτερος, -α, -ον	your		11

τίς, τί	who? which one? what?		555
τις, τι	anyone, anything; some- one, something		526
καθότι	as, because		6

ὡς	as, like, so		504
ὡσαύτως	likewise		17
ὡσεί	as, like		21
ὥσπερ	(just) as		36
ὥστε	therefore, so that		83

III. B. FAMILIES WITH ONE OR MORE WORDS OCCURRING 155-399 TIMES

1. ἄγγελος, -ου, ὁ	angel, messenger	(*angel*)	176
ἀναγγέλλω	I announce, proclaim		14
ἀπαγγέλλω	I report, proclaim		45
ἐπαγγελία, -ας, ἡ	promise		52
ἐπαγγέλλομαι	I promise		15
εὐαγγελίζομαι	I preach the Good News	(*evangelize*)	54
εὐαγγέλιον, -ου, τό	the Good News, Gospel	(*evangel*ical)	76
καταγγέλλω	I proclaim		18
παραγγέλλω	I command		32
παραγγελία, -ας, ἡ	command		5

ἅγιος, -ία, -ον	holy		233
ἁγιάζω	I make holy, sanctify		28
ἁγιασμός, -οῦ, ὁ	holiness, sanctification		10

| ἀδελφός, -οῦ, ὁ | brother | | 343 |
| *ἀδελφή, -ῆς, ἡ* | sister | | 26 |

ἀμαρτία, -ας, ἡ	sin		173
ἁμαρτάνω	I sin		43
ἁμαρτωλός, -όν	sinful		47

ἄν	(an untranslatable condi-		167
	tional particle)		
ὅταν	whenever, when		123

γῆ, γῆς, ἡ	earth	(*geology*)	250
γεωργός, -οῦ, ὁ	farmer		19
ἐπίγειος, -ον	earthly		7

2. γινώσκω   I know   (cf. *know*)   222

γνωρίζω	I make known, reveal		25
γνῶσις, -εως, ἡ	knowledge	(*gnostic*)	29
γνωστός, -ή, -όν	known		15
γνώμη, -ης, ἡ	purpose, opinion		9
ἀναγινώσκω	I read		32
ἀγνοέω	I do not know	(*agnostic*)	22
ἐπιγινώσκω	I know, understand		44
ἐπίγνωσις,	knowledge, understanding		20
-εως, ἡ			
καταγινώσκω	I condemn, convict		5
προγινώσκω	I know beforehand	(cf. *prognosis*)	5

| γράφω | I write | (*graph*) | 191 |
| *γραφή, -ῆς, ἡ* | writing | | 51 |

γράμμα, -ατος, τό	letter (of the alphabet), writing	(*grammar*)	14
γραμματεύς, -έως, ὁ	scribe		64
ἐπιγράφω	I write on		5
ἐπιγραφή, -ῆς, ἡ	inscription		5

δόξα, -ης, ἡ	glory, brightness, splendor	(*dox*ology)	166
δοξάζω	I praise, honor, glorify		61
δοκέω	I think, believe; I seem	(*doce*tism)	63
δόγμα, -ατος, τό	decree; doctrine	(*dogma*)	5
δοκιμή, -ῆς, ἡ	character		7
δόκιμος, -ον	approved, genuine		7
ἀδόκιμος, -ον	worthless		8
ἀποδοκιμάζω	I reject		9
εὐδοκέω	I am pleased with		21
εὐδοκία, -ας, ἡ	goodwill, favor		9
συνευδοκέω	I agree with, approve of		6

3. **δύναμαι**	I can	(*dynam*ic)	210
δύναμις, -εως, ἡ	power, strength	(*dynam*ite)	119
δυνατός, -ή, -όν	powerful		32
ἀδύνατος, -ον	powerless		10
ἐνδυναμόω	I strengthen; (pass.) I become strong		7

ἐκεῖνος, -η, -ο	that		265
ἐκεῖ	there, to that place		105
ἐκεῖθεν	from there		37

25

ἔργον, -ου, τό	work, deed		169
ἐργάζομαι	I work, do, accomplish		41
ἐργασία, -ας, ἡ	practice, trade		6
ἐργάτης, -ου, ὁ	workman, doer		16
ἐνέργεια, -ας, ἡ	working, action	(*energy*)	8
ἐνεργέω	I work, produce		21
καταργέω	I make ineffective, abolish		27
κατεργάζομαι	I achieve, bring about		22
λειτουργία, -ας, ἡ	service	(*liturgy*)	6
λειτουργός, -οῦ, ὁ	servant	(*liturgi*st)	5
πανουργία, -ας, ἡ	cunning, craftiness, trickery		5
συνεργέω	I cooperate		5
συνεργός, -οῦ, ὁ	helper, fellow-worker		13

---

4. ἐσθίω	I eat		158
κατεσθίω	I eat up, devour		15
συνεσθίω	I eat with		5

ἡμέρα, -ας, ἡ	day		389
σήμερον	today		41

θέλω	I wish, will		209
θέλημα, -ατος, τό	will		62

κόσμος, -ου, ὁ	the world	(*cosmos*)	186
κοσμέω	I adorn, beautify	(*cosme*tic)	10

λαλέω	I speak, say		296
καταλαλέω	I speak against, slander		5
συλλαλέω	I talk with, discuss		6

λαμβάνω	I take, receive		260
ἀναλαμβάνω	I take up		13
ἀπολαμβάνω	I receive		10
ἐπιλαμβάνομαι	I take hold of, catch		19
καταλαμβάνω	I seize, win		5
μεταλαμβάνω	I receive a share		7
παραλαμβάνω	I take, take with		50
προσλαμβάνομαι	I receive, accept		12
συλλαμβάνω	I seize, I conceive		16
ὑπολαμβάνω	I receive		5

5.
μαθητής, -οῦ, ὁ	learner, disciple	(*mathe*matics)	261
μανθάνω	I learn		25

μέγας, -άλη, -α	large, great	(*mega*ton)	243
μεγαλύνω	I make large, magnify		8

μέν	indeed, on the one hand		180
	(but often untranslatable)		
μέντοι	though, indeed		8

νόμος, -ου, ὁ	law	(anti*nom*ian)	195
νομίζω	I think, believe		15
νομικός, -ή, -όν	legal (as a noun) lawyer		9
ἀνομία, -ας, ἡ	lawlessness		15
ἄνομος, -α, -ον	lawless		10

οἶδα	I know	(*ide*a)	318
ἰδού	see!, behold!		200
ἴδε	see, here is		34
εἴδωλον, -ου, τό	image, idol	(*idol*)	11
εἰδωλόθυτος, -ον	offered to an idol		9
εἰδωλολάτρης, -ου, ὁ	idolater	(*idolater*)	7
συνείδησις, -εως, ἡ	conscience		30

6. ὄνομα, -ατος, τό name (pseudo*nym*) 231

ὄνομα, -ατος, τό	name	(pseudo*nym*)	231
ὀνομάζω	I name		10
εὐώνυμος, -ον[2]	left (as opposed to right)		9

οὐρανός, -οῦ, ὁ	heaven	(*uran*ium)	274
οὐράνιος, -ον	heavenly		9
ἐπουράνιος, -ον	heavenly		19

πιστεύω	I believe (in), trust		243
πίστις, -εως, ἡ	faith, trust		243
πιστός, -ή, -όν	faithful		67
ἀπιστέω	I disbelieve, am unfaithful		8
ἀπιστία, -ας, ἡ	unfaithfulness, unbelief		11
ἄπιστος, -η, -ον	faithless, unbelieving		23
πείθω	I convince, persuade; I trust in (cf. *faith*)		52
ἀπειθέω	I disobey, am disobedient		14
ἀπείθεια, -ας, ἡ	disobedience, disbelief		7

2. Literally "well-named," a euphemism. The ancient Greeks thought the left hand to be ill-favored.

ἀπειθής, -ές	disobedient		6

πνεῦμα, -ατος, τό	breath, spirit	(*pneum*onia)	379
πνευματικός, -ή, -όν	spiritual	(*pneuma*tic)	26
πνέω	I blow, breathe		7

---

7. τότε

τότε	then		160
πάντοτε	always		41
τοιοῦτος, -αύτη, -οῦτον	of such a kind, such as this		57
τοσοῦτος, -αύτη, -οῦτον	so great, so far, so much		20

υἱός, -οῦ, ὁ	son		379
υἱοθεσία, -ας, ἡ	adoption		5

ὑπό	(with gen.) by; (with acc.) under	(*hypo*thesis)	220
ὑποκάτω	under		11

χάρις, -ιτος, ἡ	grace, favor	(*charity*)	156
χαίρω	I rejoice, am glad		74
χαρά, -ᾶς, ἡ	joy		59
χαρίζομαι	I give freely, forgive		23
χάρισμα, -ατος, τό	a gift	(*charisma*tic)	17
εὐχαριστέω	I give thanks		38

| εὐχαριστία, -ας, ἡ | thanksgiving | (*eucharist*) | 15 |
| συγχαίρω | I rejoice with | | 7 |

III. C. FAMILIES WITH ONE OR MORE WORDS OCCURRING 100-154 TIMES

1. **ἀγαθός, -ή, -όν** — good — 102
   ἀγαθοποιέω — I do good — 9

ἀγαπάω — I love — 143
ἀγάπη, -ης, ἡ — love — 116
ἀγαπητός, -ή, -όν — beloved, dear — 61

αἴρω — I lift up; I take away — 101
ἐπαίρω — I lift up, hold up — 19

αἰών, -ῶνος, ὁ — age, eternity — (*eon*) — 122
αἰώνιος, -ον — eternal — 71
ἀεί — always — 7

ἀλήθεια, -ας, ἡ — truth, truthfulness — 109
ἀληθινός, -ή, -όν — true — 28
ἀληθής, -ές — true — 26
ἀληθῶς — truly — 18

ἀποστέλλω	I send away, send out		132
ἀπόστολος, -ου, ὁ	apostle	(*apostle*)	80
διαστέλλομαι	I order		8
ἐπιστολή, -ῆς, ἡ	letter, epistle	(*epistle*)	24
στολή, -ῆς, ἡ	robe	(*stole*)	9

ἀρχιερεύς, -έως, ὁ	high priest, chief priest		122
ἱερεύς, -έως, ὁ	priest	(*hier*archy)	31
ἱερόν, -οῦ, τό	temple		71

2.

ἀφίημι	I leave, let go, pardon		146
ἄφεσις, -έσεως, ἡ	pardon, forgiveness		17
συνίημι	I understand, comprehend		26
σύνεσις, -εως, ἡ	understanding		7

βάλλω	I throw, place	(*ball*istic)	122
διάβολος, -ου, ὁ	the devil	(*diabol*ical)	36
ἐκβάλλω	I throw out, expel		81
ἐπιβάλλω	I put around, clothe		23
καταβολή, -ῆς, ἡ	foundation		10
λιθοβολέω	I stone		7
παραβολή, -ῆς, ἡ	parable	(*parable*)	50
παρεμβολή, -ῆς, ἡ	camp, army		10
συμβάλλω	I meet, discuss; (mid.) I help		7
ὑπερβολή, -ῆς, ἡ	excess, abundance	(*hyperbole*)	8

ὑπερβάλλω	I surpass		5

βλέπω	I see, look		133
ἀναβλέπω	I look up, gain sight		25
ἐμβλέπω	I look at		12
περιβλέπομαι	I look around		7

δεῖ	it is necessary, one must		101
δέομαι	I ask		22
δέησις, -εως, ἡ	prayer, entreaty		18

δοῦλος, -ου, ὁ	slave		124
δουλεύω	I am a slave, serve		25
δουλόω	I enslave		8
δουλεία, -ας, ἡ	slavery		5
σύνδουλος, -ου, ὁ	fellow-slave		10

δύο	two	(*du*et)	132
δεύτερος, -α, -ον	second	(*Deuter*onomy)	43

3. ἐγείρω	I raise		144
γρηγορέω	I watch		22
διεγείρω	I wake (someone) up		6

ζάω	I live		140
ζωή, -ῆς, ἡ	life		135
ζῷον, -ου, τό	living thing; animal (*zoo*)		23

ζητέω	I seek, look for, ask		117
ζήτημα, -ατος, τό	question, issue		5
ζήτησις, -εως, ἡ	investigation		7
ἐκζητέω	I search for		7
ἐπιζητέω	I search for, strive for		13
συζητέω	I discuss, dispute		10

θάνατος, -ου, ὁ	death	(eu*than*asia)	120
θανατόω	I kill		11
ἀποθνῄσκω	I die		111
θνῄσκω	I die		9
θνητός, -ή, -όν	mortal		6

ἴδιος, -ία, -ον	one's own		114
ἰδιώτης, -ου, ὁ	layman, amateur	(*idiot*)	5

4. **ἴστημι**	I place, set, stand	(*sta*nd)	154
ἀνίστημι	I raise, rise, stand up		14
ἀνάστασις, -εως, ἡ	resurrection		42
ἀκαταστασία, -ας, ἡ	disturbance		5
ἀνθίστημι	I oppose, resist		14
ἀποκαθίστημι or ἀποκαθιστάνω	I restore, reestablish		8
ἀφίστημι	I go away		14
ἐνίστημι	I have come, am present		7
ἐξίστημι	I am amazed, astonished		17
ἔκστασις, -εως, ἡ	distraction, confusion; trance	(*ecstasy*)	7

33

ἐπίστασις, -εως, ἡ	pressure, burden	17
ἐφίστημι	I stand by, approach, appear	21
μεθίστημι	I remove	5
παρίστημι	I am present, stand by	41
προΐστημι	I rule, direct; I care for	8
στάσις, -εως, ἡ	uprising, revolt	8
στήκω	I stand, stand firm	10
συνίστημι or συνιστάνω	I present, introduce	16
ὑπόστασις, -εως, ἡ	substantial nature, essence	5

καλέω	I call	148
κλῆσις, -εως, ἡ	calling, position	11
κλητός, -ή, -όν	called, invited	10
ἀνέγκλητος, -ον	blameless, irreproachable	5
ἐγκαλέω	I accuse, charge	7
ἐκκλησία, -ας, ἡ	church, congregation (*ecclesi*astical)	114
ἐπικαλέω	I name; (mid.) I call upon	13
παρακαλέω	I invite; I exhort; I comfort	109
παράκλησις, -εως, ἡ	exhortation, comfort	29
παράκλητος, -ου, ὁ	mediator, helper	5
προσκαλέομαι	I call, invite	29
συγκαλέω	I call together; (mid.) I summon	8

---

5. **καλός, -ή, -όν**	good	101
καλῶς	well, beautifully	37

κρίνω	I judge		115
ἀνακρίνω	I question, examine		16
ἀποκρίνομαι	I answer, reply		232
διακρίνω	I differentiate; (mid.) I doubt		19
κατακρίνω	I condemn		18
κρίμα, -ατος, τό	judgment, condemnation		28
κρίσις, -εως, ἡ	judging, judgment	(*crisis*)	47
κριτής, -οῦ, ὁ	judge	(*crit*ic)	19
ὑποκριτής, -οῦ, -ὁ	hypocrisy	(*hypocrisy*)	6
ὑπόκρισις, -εως, ἡ	hypocrite	(*hypocrite*)	18
ἀνυπόκριτος, -ον	genuine, sincere		6

μένω	I remain, stay	(cf. re*main*)	118
διαμένω	I remain		5
ἐπιμένω	I remain, stay		17
προσμένω	I remain with, stay with		7
ὑπομένω	I remain, endure		17
ὑπομονή, -ῆς, ἡ	patience, endurance		32

νῦν	now		148
νυνί[3]	now		20

ὁδός, -οῦ, ἡ	way	(ex*odus*)	101
εἴσοδος, -ου, ἡ	entrance		5

οἶκος, -ου, ὁ	house, dwelling		114

3. An intensive form of *νῦν*, but with no difference in meaning.

οἰκία, -ας, ἡ	household		94
οἰκέω	I live, inhabit		9
ἐνοικέω	I live in		5
κατοικέω	I live, dwell in		44
οἰκοδεσπότης, -ου, ὁ	the master of the house	(*despot*)	12
οἰκονομία, -ας, ἡ	management; plan	(*economy*)	9
οἰκονόμος, -ου, ὁ	house steward	(*economist*)	10
οἰκουμένη, -ης, ἡ	the inhabited world	(*ecumen*ical)	15
οἰκονομέω	I build		40
οἰκοδομή, -ῆς, ἡ	building, edification; a building		18
ἐποικοδομέω	I build on		7

----

6. **ὀφθαλμός, -οῦ, ὁ**	eye	(*ophthalmo*logist)	100
ἐνώπιον	before		94
μέτωπον, -ου, τό	forehead		8
πρόσωπον, -ου, τό	face		76

πορεύομαι	I go, proceed		154
ἀπορέω	I am in doubt		6
εἰσπορεύομαι	I go in		18
ἐκπορεύομαι	I go out		34
ἔμπορος, -ου, ὁ	merchant	(*empor*ium)	5
παραπορεύομαι	I go by, go through		5

προφήτης, -ου, ὁ	prophet	(*prophet*)	144
προφητεύω	I prophesy		28
προφητεία, -ας, ἡ	prophecy	(*prophecy*)	19
πρόφασις, -εως, ἡ	pretext, excuse		7

φημί	I say		66
βλασφημέω	I blaspheme	(*blaspheme*)	34
βλασφημία, -ας, ἡ	blasphemy	(*blasphemy*)	18

πῶς	how?	103
πώς	somehow	15
ὅπως	(adv.) how; (conj.) that, in order that	53
πόθεν	whence?	29
ποῖος, -α, -ον	of what kind? which? what?	33
ὁποῖος, -ία, -ον	of what sort	5
πόσος, -η, -ον	how great? how much? how many?	27
ποταπός, -ή, -όν	of what sort, of what kind	7
πότε	when?	29
ποτέ	once, formerly	19
πώποτε	ever	6
ποῦ	where?	48

7. σάρξ, σαρκός, ἡ	flesh	147
σαρκικός, -ή, -όν	fleshly, in the manner of flesh	7

σῴζω	I save, deliver	107
σωτήρ, -ῆρος, ὁ	savior, deliverer	24
σωτηρία, -ας, ἡ	salvation, deliverance	46
διασῴζω	I save	8

τίθημι	I put, place	100

ἀθετέω	I reject		16
ἀνάθεμα, -ατος, τό	object of a curse	(*anathema*)	6
ἀποτίθεμαι	I put off, lay aside		9
διαθήκη, -ης, ἡ	will, testament, covenant		33
διατίθημι	I decree, make a will		7
ἐπιτίθημι	I put upon		39
παρατίθημι	I place beside, place around		19
περιτίθημι	I put around		8
πρόθεσις, -εως, ἡ	presentation; plan		12
προστίθημι	I add		18

φωνή, -ῆς, ἡ	sound, voice	(tele*phone*)	139
φωνέω	I call		43
προσφωνέω	I call at, address		7
συμφωνέω	I agree with	(*symphony*)	6

| **ψυχή, -ῆς, ἡ** | soul | (*psychiatrist*) | 103 |
| ψυχικός, -ή, -όν | unspiritual | (*psychic*) | 6 |

III. D. FAMILIES WITH ONE OR MORE WORDS OCCURRING 50-99 TIMES

1. **ἄγω**	I lead	(cf. ped*agog*ical)	67
ἀνάγω	I lead up		23
ἀπάγω	I lead away		16
εἰσάγω	I lead in		11
ἐξάγω	I lead out		12
κατάγω	I lead down		9

ὁδηγέω	I lead, guide		5
ὁδηγός, -οῦ, ὁ	leader, guide		5
παράγω	I go away, pass by		10
περιάγω	I lead around, go around		6
προάγω	I lead forward, go before		20
προσάγω	I bring, come near		5
συνάγω	I gather together		59
ἐπισυνάγω	I gather together, congregate		8
συναγωγή, -ῆς, ἡ	synagogue	(*synagogue*)	56
ὑπάγω	I go, go away		79

αἰτέω	I ask, ask for		70
αἰτία, -ας, ἡ	cause, reason		20
αἴτιος, -ία, -ον	responsible, guilty		5
παραιτέομαι	I ask for; I refuse		12

ἀνοίγω	I open		77
διανοίγω	I open, explain		8

ἀπόλλυμι	I ruin, destroy		91
ἀπώλεια, -ας, ἡ	destruction		91

2. **ἄρχω**	I rule, am first	(olig*arch*)	86
ἀρχή, -ῆς, ἡ	beginning; ruler, authority		55
ἄρχων, -οντος, ὁ	ruler, lord, authority		37
ἀρχαῖος, -α, -ον	ancient, old	(*arch*aic)	11
χιλίαρχος, -ον, ὁ	leader of a thousand soldiers, tribune		22

ἑκατοντάρχης, -ου, ὁ	centurion, captain		16
ὑπάρχω	I exist, am present		60
ἀπαρχή, -ῆς, ἡ	first-fruits		9

ἀσπάζομαι	I greet		59
ἀσπασμός, -οῦ, ὁ	greeting		10

βαπτίζω	I baptize	(*baptize*)	77
βάπτισμα, -ατος, τό	baptism	(*baptism*)	19
βαπτιστής, -οῦ, ὁ	baptist, baptizer	(*baptist*)	12

δαιμόνιον, -ου, τό	demon, evil spirit	(*demon*)	63
δαιμονίζομαι	I am demon-possessed		13

δέχομαι	I take, receive	56
ἀπεκδέχομαι	I await eagerly	8
ἀποδέχομαι	I welcome, receive	7
δεκτός, -ή, -όν	acceptable, welcome	5
προσδοκάω	I wait for	16
ἐκδέχομαι	I expect	6
παραδέχομαι	I receive	6
προσδέχομαι	I receive, welcome; I wait for	14
δεξιός, -ά, -όν	right (as opposed to left)	54
εὐπρόσδεκτος, -ον	acceptable, welcome	5

διδάσκω	I teach	(cf. *dida*ctic)	97
διδάσκαλος, -ου, ὁ	teacher		59
διδασκαλία, -ας, ἡ	teaching, instruction		21
διδαχή, -ῆς, ἡ	teaching		30

3. | **δικαιοσύνη, -ης, ἡ** | righteousness | | 92 |
δίκαιος, -α, -ον	righteous, just		79
δικαιόω	I justify		39
δικαίωμα, -ατος, τό	requirement; righteous deed		10
δικαίως	justly		5
ἀδικέω	I do wrong, treat unjustly		28
ἀδικία, -ας, ἡ	wrongdoing, unrighteousness		25
ἄδικος, -ον	unjust		12
ἀντίδικος, -ου, ὁ	opponent		5
ἐκδικέω	I avenge someone		6
ἐκδίκησις, -εως, ἡ	vengeance, punishment		9
καταδικάζω	I condemn		5

| **διό** | therefore, for this reason | | 53 |
| διότι | because, therefore | | 23 |

δώδεκα	twelve		75
δέκα	ten	(*deca*de)	24
δεκατέσσαρες	fourteen		5

| ἐλπίς, -ίδος, ἡ | hope | 53 |
| ἐλπίζω | I hope, hope for | 31 |

ἐντολή, -ῆς, ἡ	commandment, order	67
ἐντέλλομαι	I command, order	15
ἀνατέλλω	I rise up	9
ἀνατολή, -ῆς, ἡ	rising, east	11

| ἑπτά | seven | 88 |
| ἕβδομος, -η, -ον | seventh | 9 |

| ἐρωτάω | I ask, request | 63 |
| ἐπερωτάω | I ask (a question) | 56 |

---

4. | εὐθύς | immediately | 51 |
| εὐθύς, -εῖα, -ύ | straight | 8 |
| εὐθέως | immediately | 36 |

| ἤδη | now, already | 61 |
| δή | indeed, now | 5 |

| ἱμάτιον, -ου, τό | garment | 60 |
| ἱματισμός, -οῦ, ὁ | clothing | 5 |

κακός, -ή -όν	evil, bad	50
κακία, -ας, ἡ	wickedness, malice	11
κακόω	I harm, mistreat	6
κακῶς	wickedly, badly	16

42

ἐγκακέω	I become weary, lose heart	6

καρπός, -ου, ὁ	fruit	66
καρποφορέω	I bear fruit	8
ἄκαρπος, -ον	unfruitful	7

κηρύσσω	I proclaim, preach	61
κήρυγμα, -ατος, τό	proclamation, preaching	9

κράζω	I cry, call out	56
ἀνακράζω	I cry out	5

λίθος, -ου, ὁ	stone (*litho*graphy)	59
λιθάζω	I stone (a person)	9

5. **λοιπός, -ή, -όν**	remaining, other	55
λείπω	I lack, fall short	6
ἀπολείπω	I leave (behind); I remain	7
ἐγκαταλείπω	I leave behind, forsake	10
καταλείπω	I leave behind	24

ἀπολύω	I set free, let go, send away	67
λύω	I loose, set free	42
ἀπολύτρωσις, -εως, ἡ	release, redemption	10
ἐκλύομαι	(pass.) I become weary, give out	5

43

καταλύω	I destroy, abolish		17
παραλύομαι	I am disabled		5
παραλυτικός, -ή, -όν	lame; (as a noun) a paralytic	(*paralytic*)	10

| **μᾶλλον** | more, rather | | 81 |
| μάλιστα | most of all, especially | | 12 |

μαρτυρέω	I bear witness, testify		76
μαρτυρία, -ας, ἡ	testimony		37
μαρτύριον, -ον, τό	testimony, proof		19
μαρτύρομαι	I testify, affirm		5
μάρτυς, -τυρος, ὁ	witness	(*martyr*)	35
ψευδομαρτυρέω	I bear false witness		5

| **μέσος, -η, -ον** | middle, in the middle | | 58 |
| μεσίτης, -ου, ὁ | mediator | | 6 |

6. **παιδίον, -ου, τό**	infant, young child		52
παῖς, παιδός, ὁ	child	(*pedi*atrician)	24
παιδίσκη, -ης, ἡ	female slave		13
παιδεία, -ας, ἡ	upbringing, training		6
παιδεύω	I bring up, train		13
ἐμπαίζω	I ridicule, mock		13

πέμπω	I send		79
ἀναπέμπω	I send up		5
μεταπέμπομαι	I send for		9
προπέμπω	I accompany		9

περιπατέω	I go about, walk around		95
πατέω	I tread		5
καταπατέω	I trample under foot		5

πίνω	I drink		73
ποτήριον, -ου, τό	a drink	(*pot*able)	31
ποτίζω	I give a drink		15
καταπίνω	I drink down		7

πίπτω	I fall		90
ἀναπίπτω	I lie down, recline		12
ἐκπίπτω	I fall off, fall from		10
ἐμπίπτω	I fall in, fall into		7
ἐπιπίπτω	I fall upon		11
παράπτωμα, -ατος, τό	transgression, sin		20
προσπίπτω	I fall down before, fall upon		8
πτῶμα, -ατος, τό	corpse		7

---

7. πληρόω	I fill, make full, finish		87
πλήρωμα, -ατος, τό	fullness		17
πλήρης, -ες	full, complete		16
πληθύνω	I increase, multiply		12
πλῆθος, -ους, τό	crowd, multitude	(*pleth*ora)	31
ἀναπληρόω	I fill up		6
πίμπλημι	I fill, fulfill		24
ἐμπίμπλημι	I fill, satisfy		5

πλοῖον, -ου, τό	boat, ship		68
πλοιάριον, -ου, τό	small ship, boat		5
πλέω	I sail		6

πονηρός, -ά, -όν	wicked, bad		78
πονηρία, -ας, ἡ	wickedness, sinfulness		7

πούς, ποδός, ὁ	foot	(*pod*iatrist)	93
ὑποπόδιον, -ου, τό	footstool		7

προσεύχομαι	I pray		86
προσευχή, -ῆς, ἡ	prayer		37
εὔχομαι	I pray		7

πῦρ, πυρός, τό	fire	(*pyre*)	73
πυρετός, -οῦ, ὁ	fever		6
πυρόομαι	I burn, am inflamed		6

ῥῆμα, -ατος, τό	word, saying; thing, matter		68
παρρησία, -ας, ἡ	openness, confidence		31
παρρησιάζομαι	I speak freely, openly		9

σημεῖον, -ου, τό	sign		77
σημαίνω	I make known, indicate		6

| σοφία, -ας, ἡ | wisdom | (philosophy) | 51 |
| σοφός, -ή, -όν | wise | | 20 |

σπείρω	I sow		52
σπέρμα, -ατος, τό	seed	(sperm)	43
σπόρος, -ου, ὁ	seed	(spore)	6

---

8. | **τέκνον, -ου, τό** | child | | 99 |
τεκνίον, -ου, τό	little child		8
τίκτω	I give birth to		18
πρωτότοκος, -ον	first-born		8

| τηρέω | I keep, observe | | 70 |
| παρατηρέω | I watch, observe | | 6 |

τρεῖς, τρία	three	(cf. trinity)	67
τρίς	three times		12
τρίτος, -η, -ον	third		56
τριάκοντα	thirty		9

φέρω	I bear, carry	(cf. fertile)	66
ἀναφέρω	I bring up, take up		10
ἀποφέρω	I carry away		6
διαφέρω	I differ, am superior		13
εἰσφέρω	I bring in		8
ἐκφέρω	I carry out, send out		8
πληροφορέω	I fill, fulfill		6
προσφέρω	I bring to, offer		47
προσφορά, -ᾶς, ἡ	offering, gift		9

συμφέρω	I help, am profitable		15
φορέω	I bear, wear		6
φόρος, -ου, ὁ	tribute, tax		5
φορτίον, -ου, τό	burden, load		6

φοβέομαι	I fear		95
φόβος, -ου, ὁ	fear	(*pho*bia)	47
ἔμφοβος, -ον	afraid		5

φῶς, φωτός, τό	light	(*photo*graph)	73
φωτίζω	I illuminate		11
φωτεινός, -ή, -όν	shining, bright		5

III. E. FAMILIES WITH ONE OR MORE WORDS OCCURRING 26-49 TIMES

1. **ἀγοράζω**	I buy		30
ἀγορά, -ᾶς, ἡ	marketplace		11

ἀκάθαρτος, -η, -ον	impure, unclean		32
ἀκαθαρσία, -ας, ἡ	impurity, immorality		10
καθαρίζω	I make clean, purify	(cf. *cathar*sis)	31
καθαρισμός, -οῦ, ὁ	purification		7
καθαρός, -ά, -όν	clean, pure		27

ἄξιος, -ία, -ον	worthy, fit		41

ἀξιόω	I deem worthy		7
ἀξίως	worthily		6

ἀποκαλύπτω	I reveal	(*apocalyptic*)	26
ἀποκάλυψις, -εως, ἡ	revelation	(*apocalypse*)	18
καλύπτω	I cover, hide		8

ἀρνέομαι	I deny		33
ἀπαρνέομαι	I deny		11

ἀσθενέω	I am weak, sick		33
ἀσθένεια, -ας, ἡ	weakness		24
ἀσθενής, -ές	weak, powerless		26

βιβλίον, -ου, τό	book, scroll	(*biblio*graphy)	34
βίβλος, -ου, ἡ	book	(*Bible*)	10

βούλομαι	I wish, desire	(cf. *voli*tion)	37
βουλή, -ῆς, ἡ	purpose, counsel		12
βουλεύομαι	I resolve, decide		6
συμβούλιον, -ου, τό	plan, purpose		8

2. **γαμέω**	I marry	(mono*gamy*)	28
γάμος, -ου, ὁ	marriage		16
γαμίζω	I give in marriage		7

δέω	I bind, tie		43
δεσμός, -οῦ, ὁ	bond, fetter		18
δέσμιος, -ου, ὁ	prisoner		16
ὑπόδημα, -ατος, τό	sandal		10

δείκνυμι[4]	I point out, show		33
ἐνδείκνυμι	I show, demonstrate	(*indic*ation)	11
ἐπιδείκνυμι	I show, point out		7
ὑποδείκνυμι	I show, indicate		6
ὑπόδειγμα, -ατος, τό	example, pattern		6

διακονέω	I wait at table, serve		37
διακονία, -ας, ἡ	service		34
διάκονος, -ου, ὁ and ἡ	deacon	(*deacon*)	29

διώκω	I hasten; I pursue, persecute		45
διωγμός, -οῦ, ὁ	persecution		10

ἐγγίζω	I come near		42
ἐγγύς	near		31

ἐλεέω	I have mercy		29
ἔλεος, -ους, τό	mercy, compassion		27

4. This word group is closely related to that of δίκη, but for pedagogical purposes it is listed separately.

ἐλεημοσύνη, -ης, ἡ	alms	13

---

3. ἐνδύω | I clothe | 27
ἔνδυμα, -ατος, τό | garment, clothing | 8
ἐκδύω | I strip, take off | 6
δυσμή, -ῆς, ἡ | going down, west | 5

ἐπεί	because, since, for	26
ἐπειδή	since, because	10

ἐπιθυμία, -ας, ἡ | desire, longing | 38
ἐπιθυμέω | I desire, long for | 16
θυμός, -οῦ, ὁ | anger, wrath | 18
ὁμοθυμαδόν | with one mind | 11
προθυμία, -ας, ἡ | willingness, goodwill | 5

ἐπιστρέφω | I turn, turn around, turn back | 36
ἀναστρέφω | I act, live | 9
ἀναστροφή, -ῆς, ἡ | way of life, conduct | 13
διαστρέφω | I make crooked, pervert | 7
στρέφω | I turn, change | 21
ὑποστρέφω | I turn back, return | 35

ἔρημος, -ον	empty, deserted; (as a noun [ἡ]) the desert, wilderness	(*her*mit)	48
ἐρημόομαι	(pass.) I am laid waste		5

ἑτοιμάζω	I prepare	40
ἕτοιμος, -η, -ον	prepared	17

ἐχθρός, -ά, -όν	hostile; (as a noun) enemy	32
ἔχθρα, -ας, ἡ	enmity	6

4. ἡγέομαι	I lead, guide; I think		28
ἡγεμών, -όνος, ὁ	governor, procurator	(*hegemon*y)	20
διηγέομαι	I tell, relate		8
ἐξηγέομαι	I explain, interpret	(cf. *exege*sis)	6

θαυμάζω	I wonder, marvel	43
θαυμαστός, -ή, -όν	wonderful, marvelous	6

θλῖψις, -εως, ἡ	affliction, tribulation	45
θλίβω	I afflict, oppress	10

θυσία, -ας, ἡ	sacrifice, offering	28
θυσιαστήριον, -ου, τό	altar	23
θύω	I sacrifice	14
θυμίαμα, -ατος, τό	incense, incense offering	6

| ἰάομαι | I heal | | 26 |
| ἰατρός, -οῦ, ὁ | physician | (psychiatrist) | 7 |

ἰσχυρός, -ά, -όν	strong, powerful	29
ἰσχύς, -ύος, ἡ	strength, power	10
ἰσχύω	I am strong, powerful	28

καυχάομαι	I boast, glory	37
καύχημα, -ατος, τό	boast, object of boasting	11
καύχησις, -εως, ἡ	boasting	11

| κλαίω | I weep, cry | 40 |
| κλαυθμός, -οῦ, ὁ | weeping | 9 |

5.
κρατέω	I take hold of, hold fast		47
κράτος, -ους, τό	power, rule	(cf. democracy)	12
κρείττων, -ον and κρείσσων	better		19

λυπέω	I grieve; (pass.) I am sad, grieve	26
λύπη, -ης, ἡ	grief, sorrow	16
περίλυπος, -ον	very sad, deeply sorrowed	5

μέρος, -ους, τό	part	42
μερίζω	I divide, separate	14
διαμερίζω	I distribute	11
μερίς, -ίδος, ἡ	part, share	5

μετανοέω	I repent, am converted	34
μετάνοια, -ας, ἡ	repentance, conversion	22
νοέω	I perceive, understand	14
νόημα, -ατος, τό	thought, mind, design	6
νοῦς, νοός, ὁ	understanding, mind	24
νουθετέω	I admonish, instruct	8
διάνοια, -ας, ἡ	understanding, mind	12

μνημεῖον, -ου, τό	grave, tomb	40
μνῆμα, -ατος, τό	grave, tomb	8
μνεία, -ας, ἡ	remembrance, memory	7
μνημονεύω	I remember, mention	21
ἀναμιμνήσκω	I remind	6
ὑπομιμνήσκω	I remind	7

ὅμοιος, -α, -ον	like, similar	45
ὁμοίως	likewise, so, similarly	30
ὁμοιόω	I liken, compare	15
ὁμοίωμα, -ατος, τό	likeness, form	6

6. ὀπίσω	behind, back	35
ὄπισθεν	from behind	7

ὀργή, -ῆς, ἡ	anger, indignation		36
ὀργίζομαι	I am angry, indignant		8

ὀφείλω	I owe		35
ὀφειλέτης, -ου, ὁ	debtor		7

πάσχω	I suffer, endure		42
πάθημα, -ατος, τό	suffering	(em*path*y)	16

πειράζω	I test, tempt		38
πειρασμός, -οῦ, ὁ	test, temptation		21

πέντε	five	(*pent*agon)	36
πεντήκοντα	fifty		5
πεντακισχίλιοι	five thousand		6

περισσεύω	I have an abundance, am rich	39
περίσσευμα, -ατος, τό	abundance, fullness	5
περισσός, -ή, -όν	abundant, superfluous	6
περισσότερος, -α, -ον	greater, more	17
περισσοτέρως	far greater, far more, especially	12

περιτομή, -ῆς, ἡ	circumcision		36
περιτέμνω	I circumcise		17

πλανάω	I lead astray, deceive		39
πλάνη, -ης, ἡ	wandering, error, deceit		10
πλάνος, -ον	deceitful; (as a noun) deceiver, impostor		5

πλούσιος, -ία, -ον	rich		28
πλοῦτος, -ου, ὁ	riches	(*pluto*cracy)	22
πλουτέω	I am rich, become rich		12

7.

πράσσω	I do, accomplish		39
πρᾶξις, -εως, ἡ	acting, deed	(*practi*cal)	6
πρᾶγμα, -ατος, τό	deed, thing	(*pragma*tic)	11

πρό	(with gen.) before, in front of	(*pro*logue)	47
πρότερος, -α, -ον	earlier, former	(*proto*type)	11

σκανδαλίζω	I cause to fall	(*scandalize*)	29
σκάνδαλον, -ον, ὁ	that which gives offense, temptation to sin	(*scandal*)	15

σκότος, -ους, τό	darkness		31
σκοτία, -ας, ἡ	darkness		16
σκοτίζομαι	I am/become dark		5

σταυρόω	I crucify		46
σταυρός, -οῦ, ὁ	cross		27
συσταυρόω	I crucify with		5

στρατιώτης, -ου, ὁ	soldier		26
στράτευμα, -ατος, τό	army		8
στρατεύομαι	I serve in the army		7
στρατηγός, -οῦ, ὁ	praetor, captain	(*strategy*)	10

τέλος, -ους, τό	end	40
τελέω	I finish, carry out	28
τέλειος, -α, -ον	complete, perfect	19
τελειόω	I complete, perfect	23
τελευτάω	I die	13
ἐπιτελέω	I end, complete	10
συντελέω	I complete, fulfill	6
συντέλεια, -ας, ἡ	completion, close	6

τέσσαρες	four	30
τεσσαράκοντα	forty	15
τέταρτος, -η, -ον	fourth	10
τετρακισχίλιοι	four thousand	5
εἴκοσιτέσσαρες	twenty-four	6

---

8. τιμή, -ῆς, ἡ	price, value, honor	41
τίμιος, -α, -ον	valuable, precious	13

57

τιμάω	I honor		21
ἀτιμάζω	I dishonor		7
ἀτιμία, -ας, ἡ	dishonor		7
ἐπιτιμάω	I rebuke, reprove		29
ἔντιμος, -ον	honored, valuable		5

ὑποτάσσω	I subject, subordinate		38
τάσσω	I place, order		8
τάξις, -εως, ἡ	order	(syntax)	9
ἀντιτάσσομαι	I oppose		5
ἀποτάσσομαι	I say farewell, leave		6
διατάσσω	I order, direct		16
ἐπιτάσσω	I order		10
ἐπιταγή, -ῆς, ἡ	order		7
προστάσσω	I order		7

φανερόω	I reveal, make known		49
φαίνω	I shine; (mid.) I appear, become visible		31
φανερός, -ά, -όν	visible, clear		18
ἀφανίζω	I make invisible, unrecognizable		5
ἐμφανίζω	I reveal, make known		10
ἐπιφάνεια, -ας, ἡ	appearance, appearing	(epiphany)	6

φεύγω	I flee	(fugitive)	29
ἐκφεύγω	I escape		8

φίλος, -η, -ον	beloved, loving; (as a noun) friend		29
φιλέω	I love, like; I kiss		27

φίλημα, -ατος, τό	a kiss		7
καταφιλέω	I kiss		6
φιλαδελφία, -ας, ἡ	love of brother or sister		6

9. φρονέω · I think · 26
φρόνιμος, -ον · sensible, thoughtful · 14
ἄφρων, -ον · foolish, ignorant · 11
εὐφραίνω · I gladden; (pass.) I am glad · 14
καταφρονέω · I despise, scorn · 9
σωφρονέω · I am in sound mind · 6

φυλακή, -ῆς, ἡ	watch, guard	(prophylactic)	47
φυλάσσω	I watch, guard		31
γαζοφυλακεῖον, -ον, τό	treasure room, treasury		5

φυλή, -ῆς, ἡ	tribe, nation	(*phylum*)	31
φύσις, -εως, ἡ	nature		14
φυτεύω	I plant		11

χρεία, -ας, ἡ	need, necessity		49
χράομαι	I use		11
χρῄζω	I need		5
χρῆμα, -ατος, τό	property, money		6
χρηματίζω	I reveal; I bear a name		9
χρηστός, -ή, -όν	useful		7

| χρηστότης, -ητος, ἡ | goodness, usefulness | | 10 |
| παραχρῆμα | immediately | | 18 |

| χρόνος, -ου, ὁ | time | (*chron*icle) | 49 |
| χρονίζω | I take time, delay | | 5 |

χώρα, -ας, ἡ	country, land	28
χωρέω	I make room, give away	10
χωρίον, -ου, τό	place, land, field	10

| χωρίς | without, apart from | 41 |
| χωρίζω | I divide, separate | 13 |

III. F. FAMILIES WITH ONE OR MORE WORDS OCCURRING 10-25 TIMES

| 1. ἀγαλλιάω | I exult, am glad | 11 |
| ἀγαλλίασις, -εως, ἡ | exultation, joy | 5 |

| ἀμπελών, -ῶνος, ὁ | vineyard | 23 |
| ἄμπελος, -ου, ἡ | vine | 9 |

| ἀνά | (with acc.) up; (with numbers) each, apiece | 13 |
| ἄνωθεν | from above, again | 13 |

ἄνω	above, upward		9
ἐπάνω	above, over		19

ἀνάγκη, -ης, ἡ	necessity, distress		18
ἀναγκάζω	I compel		9
ἀναγκαῖος, -α, -ον	necessary		8

ἀναιρέω	I take away, destroy		24
ἀφαιρέω	I take away		10
ἐξαιρέω	I take out; (mid.) I free		8
καθαιρέω	I tear down, destroy		9
αἵρεσις, -εως, ἡ	party, dissension	(*heresy*)	9

ἀναχωρέω	I go away, take refuge		14
περίχωρος, -ον	neighboring; (as a noun) neighborhood		9

ἅπαξ	once		14
ἐφάπαξ	once for all		5

ἀργύριον, -ου, τό	silver	(*Argentina*)	20
ἄργυρος, -ου, ὁ	silver		5

ἀρέσκω	I please		17
ἀρεστός, -ή, -όν	pleasing		5
εὐάρεστος, -ον	pleasing, acceptable		9

2. ἁρπάζω	I seize, steal		14
ἅρπαξ, -αγος	rapacious; (as a noun) robber		5

ἀστήρ, -έρος, ὁ	star	(*astr*onomy)	24
ἀστραπή, -ῆς, ἡ	lightning		9

βασανίζω	I torture, torment		12
βασανισμός, -οῦ, ὁ	torture, tormenting		6

βοάω	I call, shout		12
βοηθέω	I aid, help		8

βρῶμα, -ατος, τό	food		17
βρῶσις, -εως, ἡ	eating, rust, food		11

γέμω	I am full		11
γεμίζω	fill		8

γόνυ, -ατος, τό	knee		12
γωνία, -ας, ἡ	corner	(tri*gon*ometry)	9

δεῦτε	come (on)!		12
δεῦρο	come, come here		9

ἐκκόπτω	I cut off, cut down		10
ἀποκόπτω	I cut off		6
ἐγκόπτω	I hinder, thwart		5
κόπτω	I cut		8
προκόπτω	I progress		6
προσκόπτω	I take offense at		8
πρόσκομμα, -ατος, τό	stumbling, offense		6

3. ἕκτος, -η, -ον	sixth		14
ἕξ	six	(six)	10
ἐξήκοντα	sixty		6

ἐλαία, -ας, ἡ	olive tree	13
ἔλαιον, -ου, τό	oil	11

ἐντεῦθεν	from here	10
ἐνθάδε	here	8

ἔπαινος, -ου, ὁ	praise	11
ἐπαινέω	I praise	6
αἰνέω	I praise	8

ἐπαύριον	tomorrow	17
αὔριον	tomorrow	14

ἔπειτα	then	16
εἶτα	then, next	15

ἐπισκέπτομαι	I oversee, care for		11
ἐπίσκοπος, -ου, ὁ	overseer, bishop	(*episcop*al)	5
σκοπέω	I look out for, notice		6

ἐπιτρέπω	I permit		18
ἐκτρέπομαι	I turn, turn away		5
ἐντρέπω	I shame; (mid.) I respect		9
τρόπος, -ου, ὁ	manner, kind		13

εὐσέβεια, -ας, ἡ	piety, godliness		15
σέβομαι	I worship		10
ἀσέβεια, -ας, ἡ	ungodliness, impiety		6
ἀσεβής, -ές	godless, impious		9

4. ζῆλος, -ου, ὁ and *ζῆλος, -ους, τό*	zeal, jealousy	(*zeal*)	16
ζηλόω	I am zealous, jealous		11
ζηλωτής, -οῦ, ὁ	zealot	(*zealot*)	8

ζύμη, -ης, ἡ	yeast, leaven	(en*zyme*)	13
ἄζυμος, -ον	unleavened		9

θεμέλιος, -ου, ὁ	foundation		15
θεμέλιον, -ου, τό	foundation		11
θεμελιόω	I lay a foundation		5

θερίζω	I harvest		21
θερισμός, -οῦ, ὁ	harvest		13

θησαυρός, **-οῦ, ὁ**	treasure	(*thesaurus*)	17
θησαυρίζω	I store up		8

καίω	I burn	12
κατακαίω	I burn down, consume	12

καταισχύνω	I put to shame, dishonor	13
αἰσχύνομαι	I am ashamed	5
αἰσχύνη, -ης, ἡ	shame	6
ἐπαισχύνομαι	I am ashamed	11

κατηγορέω	I accuse	(cf. *categori*cal)	23
κατήγορος, -ου, *ὁ*	accuser		5

κεῖμαι	I lie, recline	24
ἀνάκειμαι	I lie, recline	14
συνανάκειμαι	I recline with	7
ἀντίκειμαι	I am opposed	8
ἐπίκειμαι	I lie upon, press upon	7
κατάκειμαι	I lie down	12
κοιμάομαι	I sleep, fall asleep, die	18
περίκειμαι	I lie around; I wear	5
πρόκειμαι	I lie before, am present	5

5. κενός, -ή, -όν empty 18
κενόω I empty 5

κλάω I break 14
κλάσμα, -ατος, fragment 9
τό
κλάδος, -ου, ὁ branch 11

κλείω I shut, lock 16
κλείς, -δός, ἡ key 6

κλέπτης, -ου, ὁ thief (*klept*omaniac) 16
κλέπτω I steal 13

κληρονομέω I inherit, acquire 18
κληρονομία, inheritance, possession 14
-ας, ἡ
κληρονόμος, heir 15
-ου, ὁ
κλῆρος, -ου, ὁ lot, share 11

κοινωνία, -ας, ἡ communion, fellowship, 19
participation
κοινωνέω I share, participate 8
κοινωνός, -οῦ, companion, partner 10
ὁ and ἡ
κοινός, -ή, -όν communal, common 14
κοινόω I make common, defile 14

κοπιάω	I work		23
κόπος, -ου, ὁ	trouble, work		18
εὐκοπώτερος, -ον	easier		7

κρύπτω	I hide	(*crypt*)	19
κρυπτός, -ή, -όν	hidden, secret		17

κτίσις, -εως, ἡ	creation, creature		19
κτίζω	I create		15

λατρεύω	I serve	(cf. ido*later*)	21
λατρεία, -ας, ἡ	service, worship		5

λύχνος, -ου, ὁ	lamp		14
λυχνία, -ας, ἡ	lampstand		12

6. μακροθυμία, -ας, ἡ	patience, steadfastness		14
μακροθυμέω	I wait patiently		10
μακράν	far away		10
μακρόθεν	from far away		5
μακρός, -ά, -όν	long		14

μέλει	it is a care		10
μεταμέλομαι	I regret, repent		6

67

μεριμνάω	I am anxious; I care for		19
μέριμνα, -ης, ή	anxiety, care		6

μέτρον, -ου, τό	measure	(*metr*ic)	14
μετρέω	I measure		11

μοιχεύω	I commit adultery		15
μοιχαλίς, -ίδος, ή	adulteress		7

μωρός, -ά, -όν	foolish, stupid	(*moron*)	12
μωρία, -ας, ή	foolishness		5

νέος, -α, -ον	new, young		24
νεανίσκος, -ου, ό	youth, young man		11

νηστεύω	I fast		20
νηστεία, -ας, ή	fasting		6

νυμφίος, -ου, ό	bridegroom		16
νύμφη, -ης, ή	bride	(*nymph*)	8

ξένος, -η, -ον	strange, foreign		14
ξενίζω	I entertain; I surprise		10

ξηραίνω	I dry, dry up		15
ξηρός, -ά, -όν	dry	(*xero*graphy)	8

ὅριον, -ου, τό	region		12
ὁρίζω	I determine, appoint	(*horiz*on)	8
προορίζω	I predestine		6

7. **παλαιός, -ά, -όν**	old	(*paleo*lithic)	19
πάλαι	long ago, for a long time		7

παύω	I cease	15
ἀναπαύω	I give rest, refresh	12
ἀνάπαυσις, -εως, ἡ	rest, resting place	5
κατάπαυσις, -εως, ἡ	rest, resting place	9

πενθέω	I grieve, mourn	10
πένθος, -ους, τό	grief, mourning	5

πέραν	across	23
διαπεράω	I cross over	6

πετεινόν, -οῦ, τό	bird	14
πέτομαι	I fly	5

πλεονεξία, -ας, ἡ	greediness, covetousness	10
πλεονάζω	I am/become more; I increase	9
πλεονεκτέω	I take advantage, outwit	5

πληγή, -ῆς, ἡ	blow, wound	(*plague*)	22
ἐπιπλήσσω	I strike, reprove		13

ποιμήν, -ένος, ὁ	shepherd		18
ποιμαίνω	I tend, pasture		11
ποίμνη, -ης, ἡ	flock		5
ποίμνιον, -ου, τό	flock		5

πόλεμος, -ου, ὁ	war	(*polemics*)	18
πολεμέω	I make war		7

πορνεία, -ας, ἡ	prostitution, unchastity	(*porn*ography)	25
πορνεύω	I practice prostitution, am sexually immoral		8
πόρνη, -ης, ἡ	prostitute		12
πόρνος, -ου, ὁ	a sexually immoral person		10

8. **πυλών, -ῶνος, ὁ**	gate, gateway		18
πύλη, -ης, ἡ	gate, door		10

σαλπίζω	I trumpet		12
σάλπιγξ, -ιγγος, ἡ	trumpet		11

σεισμός, -οῦ, ὁ	shaking, earthquake	(*seis*mic)	14
σείω	I shake, agitate		5

σκεῦος, -ους, τό	vessel, jar		23
κατασκευάζω	I prepare, furnish		11
παρασκευή, -ῆς, ἡ	preparation		6

| σκηνή, -ῆς, ἡ | tent, dwelling, tabernacle | (scene) | 20 |
| σκηνόω | I live, dwell | | 5 |

| σπλαγχνίζομαι | I feel sympathy for | | 12 |
| σπλάγχνον, -ου, τό | heart; love, sympathy | | 11 |

9.

σπουδή, -ῆς, ἡ	haste; eagerness		12
σπουδάζω	I hasten; I am eager		11
σπεύδω	I hasten		6

| σφραγίς, -ῖδος, ἡ | seal | | 16 |
| σφραγίζω | I seal | | 15 |

| σχίζω | I split, divide | (schizophrenia) | 11 |
| σχίσμα, -ατος, τό | split, division | (schism) | 8 |

ταπεινόω	I make low, humble		14
ταπεινός, -ή, -όν	lowly, humble		8
ταπεινοφροσύνη, -ης, ἡ	humility		7

ταχέως	quickly		15
τάχος, -ους, τό	speed, quickness		8
ταχύς, -εῖα, -ύ	quick		13

9.
τυγχάνω	I meet, happen		12
ἐντυγχάνω	I appeal to		5
ἐπιτυγχάνω	I obtain, attain to		5

τύπος, -ου, ὁ	image, copy	(*type*)	15
τύπτω	I strike, beat		13

ὑγιαίνω	I am healthy, sound	(cf. *hygiene*)	12
ὑγιής, -ές	healthy, sound		12

ὑστερέω	I am in need, fail; (pass.) I lack		16
ὑστέρημα	need		9
ὕστερος, -α, -ον	second, later, finally		12

ὑψόω	I lift up		20
ὑψηλός, -ή, -όν	high		11
ὕψιστος, -η, -ον	highest, most exalted		13
ὕψος, -ους, τό	height		6

φονεύω	I murder, kill		12
φόνος, -ου, ὁ	murder, killing		9
φονεύς, -έως, ὁ	murderer		7

χιλιάς, -άδος, ἡ	(a group of) a thousand		23
χίλιοι, -αι, -α	thousands		8

χορτάζω	I feed, fill; (pass.) I eat my fill		16
χόρτος, -ου, ὁ	grass, hay		15

χρυσοῦς, -ῆ, -οῦν	golden		18
χρυσίον, -ου, τό	gold		12
χρυσός, -οῦ, ὁ	gold		10

ψεύδομαι	I lie	(*pseudo*nym)	12
ψεῦδος, -ους, τό	lie		10
ψεύστης, -ου, ὁ	liar		10
ψευδοπροφήτης, -ου, ὁ	false prophet		11

III. G. FAMILIES WITH ONE OR MORE WORDS OCCURRING 5-9 TIMES

1. ἁγνός, -ή, -όν	pure, holy		8
ἁγνίζω	I purify		7

ἀγωνίζομαι	I struggle, fight		8
ἀγών, -ῶνος, ὁ	contest, fight	(cf. *agony*)	6

ἅλας, -ατος, τό	salt		8
ἁλιεύς, -έως, ὁ	fisherman		5

ἀλείφω	I anoint		9
ἐξαλείφω	I wipe away, remove		5

ἀπάτη, -ης, ἡ	deception, deceitfulness		7
ἐξαπατάω	I deceive, cheat		6

βαρέω	I weigh down, burden	(*baro*meter)	6
βάρος, -ους, τό	weight, burden		6
βαρύς, -εῖα, -ύ	heavy		6

βέβαιος, -α, -ον	firm, permanent		8
βεβαιόω	I make firm, establish		8

διαρ(ρ)ήγνυμι or **διαρήσσω**	I tear, break		7
ῥήγνυμι	I tear, break		5

διασκορπίζω	I scatter, disperse		9
σκορπίος, -ου, ὁ	scorpion	(*scorpion*)	5

διατρίβω	I spend; I stay		9
συντρίβω	I shatter, break		7

ἐπιλανθάνομαι	I forget	8
λανθάνω	I am hidden	6

ἔρις, -ιδος, ἡ	strife, discord	9
ἐριθεία, -ας, ἡ	strife; selfishness	7

2.

ζώνη, -ης, ἡ	belt, girdle	8
περιζώννυμι	I gird about	6

θαρσέω	I am courageous, cheerful	7
θαρρέω	I am confident, courageous	6

κλίνη, -ης, ἡ	bed, couch (cf. recline)	9
ἀνακλίνω	I cause to lie down; (pass.) I lie down	6
κατακλίνω	I cause to lie down; (pass.) I lie down	5
πρωτοκλισία, -ας, ἡ	the place of honor	5

κόκκος, -ου, ὁ	seed, grain	7
κόκκινος, -η, -ον	red, scarlet	6

κραυγάζω	I cry out, shout	9
κραυγή, -ῆς, ἡ	cry, shout	6

λαμπάς, **-άδος, ἡ**	torch, lamp	(*lamp*)	9
λαμπρός, -ά, -όν	bright, shining		9
λάμπω	I shine, shine out		7

μαστιγόω	I whip, scourge	7
μάστιξ, -ιγος, ἡ	scourging, torment	6

3.
μεθερμηνεύω	I translate	(cf. *hermeneu*tics)	8
διερμηνεύω	I explain, translate		6

μετασχηματίζω	I transform	6
εὐσχήμων, -ον	prominent, of high repute	5

ὀκτώ	eight	(*octo*pus)	6
ὄγδοος, -η, -ον	eighth		5

ὀνειδίζω	I reproach, insult	9
ὀνειδισμός, -οῦ, ὁ	reproach, insult	5

ὀξύς, -εῖα, -ύ	sharp	8
ὄξος, -ους, τό	sour wine, vinegar	6

σκιά, -ᾶς, ἡ	shade, shadow	7
ἐπισκιάζω	I overshadow, cover	5

| σκληρύνω | I harden | (multiple *sclero*sis) | 6 |
| σκληρός, -ά, -όν | hard, difficult | | 5 |

| στοιχεῖον, -ου, τό | element; heavenly body | | 7 |
| στοιχέω | I hold to, follow | | 5 |

φθείρω	I destroy, ruin		9
φθαρτός, -ή, -όν	perishable, corruptible		6
ἄφθαρτος, -η, -ον	imperishable, incorruptible		8
ἀφθαρσία, -ας, ἡ	incorruptibility, immortality		7
διαφθείρω	I destroy, ruin		6
διαφθορά, -ᾶς, ἡ	destruction, corruption		6
φθορά, -ᾶς, ἡ	destruction		9

| χρίω | I anoint | | 5 |
| ἀντίχριστος, -ου, ὁ | the antichrist[5] | (*antichrist*) | 5 |

| ψαλμός, -οῦ, ὁ | song of praise, psalm | (*psalm*) | 7 |
| ψάλλω | I sing | | 5 |

| ᾠδή, -ῆς, ἡ | song | (*ode*) | 7 |
| ᾄδω | I sing | | 5 |

5. Note that the proper noun Χριστός, "Messiah, Christ," is also a member of this word family.

77

Part Four

New Testament Greek Vocabulary without Cognate, Listed by Frequency

IV. A. WORDS OCCURRING 400 OR MORE TIMES

ἀπό	(with gen.) from, away from		646
γάρ	for		1042
δέ	but, and (frequently untranslated)		2801
διά	(with gen.) through; (with acc.) because of, for the sake of	(*dia*meter)	668
ἐν	(with dat.) in	(cf. *in*)	2757
ἐπί	(with gen.) over, upon; (with dat.) on, in; (with acc.) on, against	(*epi*graph)	891
θεός, -οῦ, ὁ	God, god	(*theo*logy)	1318
οὖν	therefore, then		501

IV. B. WORDS OCCURRING 155-399 TIMES

ἀνήρ, -δρός, ὁ	man	(*andro*gen)	216
γυνή, -αικός, ἡ	woman	(*gyneco*logist)	215
ἔθνος, -ους, τό	nation, the Gentiles	(*ethn*ic)	162
εὑρίσκω	I find, discover	(*heuris*tic)	176
ἤ	or, either		344
εἷς, μία, ἕν[1]	one		346
ὄχλος, -ου, ὁ	multitude		175
παρά	(with gen.) from; (with dat.) at, by; (with acc.) by, near	(*para*medic)	194
πόλις, -εως, ἡ	city	(*polit*ics)	164
πρῶτος, -η, -ον	first	(*proto*type)	156
τέ	and		215
χείρ, χειρός, ἡ	hand		178

IV. C. WORDS OCCURRING 100-154 TIMES

ἀμήν	so let it be, truly, amen	(*amen*)	130
ἕως	until		146
καρδία, -ας, ἡ	heart	(*cardi*ologist)	151
λαός, -οῦ, ὁ	people	(cf. *lai*ty)	142
μέλλω	I am about to, intend		109
μόνος, -η, -ον	only, alone	(*mono*graph)	11
νεκρός, -ά, -όν	dead	(*necro*logy)	128
ὅλος, -η, -ον	whole, complete	(*holo*gram)	110
πάλιν	again		141
σύν	(with dat.) with	(*syn*tax)	128

1. These three gender-forms of "one" are in reality three separate words, as can readily be seen from their different forms. Each has its own cognates, e.g., οὐδείς, οὐδεμία, οὐδέν, respectively. They are shown together here to aid memorization.

σῶμα, -ατος, τό	body	(psychosomatic)	142
ὑπέρ	(with gen.) on behalf of; (with acc.) above	(hyperactive)	100
ὥρα, -ας, ἡ	hour	(horoscope)	106

IV. D. WORDS OCCURRING 50-99 TIMES

αἷμα, -ατος, τό	blood	(hemoglobin)	97
ἀκολουθέω	I follow	(acolyte)	90
ἀποκτείνω	I kill		74
ἄρτος, -ου, ὁ	bread		97
γλῶσσα, -ης, ἡ	tongue, language	(glossolalia)	50
εἰρήνη, -ης, ἡ	peace	(irenic)	92
ἕκαστος, -η, -ον	each, every		82
ἔσχατος, -η, -ον	last	(eschatology)	52
ἕτερος, -α, -ον	other, another, different	(heterosexual)	99
ἔτι	yet, still		93
θάλασσα, -ης, ἡ	sea		91
θεωρέω	I see, perceive	(cf. theory)	58
θρόνος, -ου, ὁ	throne	(throne)	62
καιρός, -οῦ, ὁ	time, right time		86
κεφαλή, -ῆς, ἡ	head	(encephalitis)	75
μακάριος, -α, -ον	blessed, happy		50
μήτηρ, -τρός, ἡ	mother	(maternal)	83
νύξ, νυκτός, ἡ	night		61
ὄρος, -ους, τό	mountain, hill		63
πρεσβύτερος, -α, -ον	old; (as a noun) elder	(presbyterian)	66
προσκυνέω	I worship		60
σάββατον, -ου, τό	Sabbath, week	(Sabbath)	68
στόμα, -ατος, τό	mouth	(stomach)	78
τόπος, -ου, ὁ	place	(topography)	94
τυφλός, -ή, -όν	blind		50

| ὕδωρ, -ατος, τό | water | (*hydro*electric) | 78 |

IV. E. WORDS OCCURRING 26-49 TIMES

1.

ἅπτω	I kindle; I touch, hold		39
ἄρα	so, then		49
ἀρνίον, -ου, τό	sheep, lamb		30
ἄρτι	now, just		36
ἄχρι	until		49
βαστάζω	I bear		27
γέ	(usually untranslatable particle, emphasizing the word it follows)		28
ἥκω	I have come, am present		26
ἥλιος, -ου, ὁ	sun		32
θεραπεύω	I care for, heal	(*therapeu*tic)	43
θηρίον, -ου, τό	animal		46
θυγάτηρ, -τρός, ἡ	daughter		28
θύρα, -ας, ἡ	door		39
ἱκανός, -ή, -όν	sufficient, large		39
κελεύω	I command, urge		26
κώμη, -ης, ἡ	village		27

2.

μάχαιρα, -ης, ἡ	sword		29
μέλος, -ους, τό	member, part		34
μικρός, -ά, -όν	small	(*micro*be)	46
μισέω	I hate	(*mis*anthrope)	40
μισθός, -οῦ, ὁ	wages		29
μυστήριον, -ου, τό	mystery, secret rites	(*mystery*)	28
ναί	yes, indeed		33

81

νικάω	I conquer		28
οἶνος, -ου, ὁ	wine	(cf. *wine*)	34
ὀλίγος, -η, -ον	few, little		41
ὀμνύω /ὄμνυμι	I swear, take an oath		26
οὐαί	woe, alas		47
οὖς, ὠτός, τό	ear		37
πλήν	but, except		31
πτωχός, -ή, -όν	poor		34
χήρα, -ας, ἡ	widow		27

IV. F. WORDS OCCURRING 10-25 TIMES

1. ἄκανθα, -ης, ἡ	thorn-plant		14
ἀκροβυστία, -ας, ἡ	uncircumcision, the Gentiles		20
ἀλέκτωρ, -ορος, ὁ	cock		12
ἄλυσις, -εως, ἡ	chain		11
ἅμα	together		10
ἀμφότεροι, -αι,-α	both, all		14
ἀντί	(with gen.) in place of, for		22
ἀριθμός, -οῦ, ὁ	number	(*arithm*etic)	18
ἀσέλγεια, -ας, ἡ	licentiousness, sensuality		10
ἀσκός, -οῦ, ὁ	wine-skin		12
αὐξάνω	I grow, increase		23
ἀφορίζω	I separate	(*aphorism*)	10
βροντή, -ῆς, ἡ	thunder	(*bronto*saurus)	12
γέεννα, -ης, ἡ	Gehenna, hell	(*gehenna*)	12
γεύομαι	I taste; I come to know		15
γυμνός, -ή, -όν	naked	(*gymn*asium)	15
δάκρυον, -ου, τό	tear		10
δεῖπνον, -ου, τό	dinner, supper		16

δένδρον, -ου, τό	tree		25
δέρω	I beat		15
δεσπότης, -ου, ὁ	lord, master	(*despot*)	10
δηνάριον, -ου, τό	denarius	(*denarius*)	16
δίκτυον, -ου, τό	net		12
διψάω	I thirst		16
δόλος, -ου, ὁ	deceit		11
δράκων, -οντος, ὁ	dragon	(*dragon*)	13

2. ἐάω	I permit; I let go, leave alone		11
ἔθος, -ους, τό	custom, law	(*ethic*)	12
εἰκών, -όνος, ἡ	image	(*icon*)	23
ἐλάχιστος, -ίστη, -ιστον	smallest, least		14
ἐλέγχω	I expose, convict, convince		17
ἔνατος, -η, -ον	ninth		10
ἕνεκεν or ἕνεκα	(with gen.) because of, for the sake of		19
ἐνιαυτός, -οῦ, ὁ	year		14
ἔνοχος, -ον	liable, guilty		10
ἐπίσταμαι	I know, understand		14
θεάομαι	I see		22
θρίξ, τριχός, ἡ	hair		15
ἵππος, -ου, ὁ	horse	(*hippo*potamus)	17
ἰχθύς, -ύος, ὁ	fish		20
κάλαμος, -ου, ὁ	reed		12
καπνός, -οῦ, ὁ	smoke		13
κέρας, -ατος, τό	horn	(tri*cera*tops)	11
κερδαίνω	I gain		17
κοιλία, -ας, ἡ	womb, belly		22
κολλάομαι	I cling to, join		12
κράβαττος, -ου, ὁ	mattress, bed		11

κωλύω	I hinder, forbid		23
κωφός, -ή, -όν	mute, deaf		14
λευκός, -ή, -όν	white	(*leuk*emia)	25
λῃστής, -οῦ, ὁ	robber		15
λίαν	very (much)		12
λίμνη, -ης, ἡ	lake		11
λιμός, -οῦ, ἡ	hunger, famine		12

3.

μέχρι	until		17
μήν, μηνός, ὁ	month	(*meno*pause)	18
μύρον, -ου, τό	ointment, perfume		14
νεφέλη, -ης, ἡ	cloud		25
νήπιος, -ία, -ιον	infant, minor		15
νίπτω	I wash		17
νόσος, -ου, ἡ	disease, illness		11
ξύλον, -ου, τό	wood, tree; cross	(*xylo*phone)	20
ὀδούς, ὀδόντος, ὁ	tooth	(ortho*dont*ist)	12
ὅρκος, -ου, ὁ	oath		10
ὄφις, -εως, ὁ	snake, serpent		14
παρθένος, -ου, ἡ and ὁ	virgin	(the *Parthen*on)	15
πατάσσω	I strike		10
πεινάω	I hunger		23
περιστερά, -ᾶς, ἡ	pigeon, dove		10
πέτρα, -ας, ἡ	rock, stone	(*Peter*)	15
πηγή, -ῆς, ἡ	spring, fountain		11
πιάζω	I seize, catch		12
πλησίον	near		17
ποικίλος, -η, -ον	manifold		10
ποταμός, -οῦ, ὁ	river, stream	(hippo*potamus*)	17
πραΰτης, -ητος, ἡ	gentleness, humility, meekness		11
πρίν	before		13
προσκαρτερέω	I hold fast to		10

πρωΐ	early (in the morning)		12
πυνθάνομαι	I ask		12
πωλέω	I sell	(monopoly)	22
πῶλος, -ου, ἡ	ass's foal, young donkey		12

4.

ῥαββί	rabbi	(*rabbi*)	15
ῥάβδος, -ου, ἡ	rod, staff		12
ῥίζα, -ης, ἡ	root		17
ῥύομαι	I save		17
σαλεύω	I shake		15
σιγάω	I am silent, still		10
σῖτος, -ου, ὁ	wheat, grain		14
σιωπάω	I am silent		10
στέφανος, -ου, ὁ	crown	(*Stephen*)	18
στηρίζω	I establish, strengthen		13
σφάζω	I slaughter		10
σφόδρα	very (much)		11
τάλαντον, -ου, τό	talent	(*talent*)	14
ταράσσω	I trouble		18
τελώνης, -ου, ὁ	tax collector		21
τέρας, -ατος, τό	wonder		16
τολμάω	I dare		16
τράπεζα, -ης, ἡ	table		15
τρέχω	I run		20
ὑπηρέτης, -ου, ὁ	servant, assistant		20
φείδομαι	I spare		10
φιάλη, -ης, ἡ	bowl	(*vial*)	12
χείρων, -ον	worse		11
χιτών, -ῶνος, ὁ	tunic		11
χορός, -ου, ὁ	swine		12
χωλός, -ή, -όν	lame		14
ὤ	O! Oh!		17
ὠφελέω	I help		15

IV. G. WORDS OCCURRING 5-9 TIMES

1. | ἄβυσσος, -ου, ἡ | abyss, underworld | (*abyss*) | 9 |
   |---|---|---|---|
   | ἀγανακτέω | I am indignant | | 7 |
   | ἀγέλη, -ης, ἡ | herd | | 7 |
   | ἀετός, -οῦ, ὁ | eagle | | 5 |
   | ἀήρ, ἀέρος, ὁ | air | (*air*) | 7 |
   | αἰγιαλός, -οῦ, ὁ | shore | | 6 |
   | ἀκριβῶς | accurately, carefully | | 9 |
   | ἄκρον, -ου, τό | high point, limit | | 6 |
   | ἄμμος, -ου, ἡ | sand | | 5 |
   | ἄμωμος, -ον | unblemished, blameless | | 8 |
   | ἀνθύπατος, -ου, ὁ | proconsul | | 5 |
   | ἁπλότης, -ητος, ἡ | sincerity | | 8 |
   | ἀποδημέω | I journey | | 6 |
   | ἀποθήκη, -ης, ἡ | storehouse, barn | (*apothe*cary) | 6 |
   | ἀποστερέω | I steal | | 6 |
   | ἀπωθέομαι | I repudiate | | 6 |
   | ἀργός, -ή, -όν | idle | | 8 |
   | ἀρετή, -ῆς, ἡ | virtue | | 5 |
   | ἀρκέω | I am enough, suffice | | 8 |
   | ἄρρωστος, -ον | sick | | 5 |
   | ἄρσην, -ενος, ὁ | male | | 9 |
   | ἀσύνετος, -ον | foolish | | 5 |
   | ἀσφαλής, -ές | safe, firm | | 5 |
   | ἀφορμή, -ῆς, ἡ | occasion, opportunity | | 7 |
   | βάθος, -ους, τό | depth | | 8 |
   | βάρβαρος, -ον | strange, foreign | (*barbar*ian) | 6 |
   | βάτος, -ου, ἡ | thornbush | | 6 |
   | βδέλυγμα, -ατος, τό | abomination | | 6 |

2. | βόσκω | I tend, feed | | 9 |
   |---|---|---|---|
   | βοῦς, -ός, ὁ | ox; (fem.) cow | (cf. *bo*vine) | 8 |
   | βραχύς, -εῖα, -ύ | short, little | | 7 |

βρέφος, -ους, τό	baby		8
βρέχω	I send rain		7
βρυγμός, -οῦ, ὁ	gnashing		7
βύσσινος, -η, -ον	made of fine linen		5
γάλα, -ακτος, τό	milk	(*gala*xy)	5
γαστήρ, -τρός, ἡ	belly, womb	(*gastr*ic)	9
γογγύζω	I murmur		8
δάκτυλος, -ου, ὁ	finger	(ptero*dactyl*)	8
δαπανάω	I spend freely		5
δηλόω	I make clear		7
δίς	twice	(cf. *di-*)	6
δοκός, -οῦ, ἡ	beam		6
δρέπανον, -ου, τό	sickle		8
δῶμα, -ατος, τό	roof, housetop		7
ἐγκεντρίζω	I graft		6
εἰκῇ	in vain		6
ἐλαύνω	I drive, row		5
ἕλκω	I draw		8
ἐμβριμάομαι	I warn; I am deeply moved		5
ἐμπτύω	I spit on (or) at		6
ἐραυνάω	I search, examine		6
ἐκμάσσω	I wipe		5
ἐκτείνω	extend		9
ἐπιεικής, -ές	gentle		6
ἐσθής, -ῆτος, ἡ	clothing		8
εὖ	well	(*eu*logy)	6
ἔχιδνα, -ης, ἡ	viper		5

3. ζημιόομαι	I forfeit		6
ζιζάνιον, -ου, τό	weed		8
ζόφος, -ου, ὁ	darkness		5
ζυγός, -οῦ, ὁ	yoke		6
ἡλικία, -ας, ἡ	age, stature		8
ἥμισυς, -εια, -υ	half	(*hemi*sphere)	5
ἡσυχάζω	I am quiet		5

θερμαίνομαι	I warm myself	(cf. *therm*ometer)	6
θόρυβος, -ου, ὁ	noise, turmoil		7
θώραξ, -ακος, ὁ	breastplate	(*thorax*)	5
ἴσος, -η, -ον	equal	(*iso*metrics)	8
κάμηλος, -ου, ὁ	camel	(*camel*)	6
καταπέτασμα, -ατος, τό	curtain		6
κατηχέω	I teach	(*catech*ize)	8
κῆπος, -ου, ὁ	garden		5
κιβωτός, -οῦ, ἡ	ark		6
κίνδυνος, -ου, ὁ	danger		9
κινέω	I move	(*kine*tic)	8
κολαφίζω	I strike		5
κόλπος, -ου, ὁ	breast, chest		6
κονιορτός, -οῦ, ὁ	dust		5

4. κοράσιον, -ου, τό	little girl		8
κόφινος, -ου, ὁ	basket		6
κράσπεδον, -ου, τό	hem, tassel		5
κρεμάννυμι	I hang		7
κρούω	I knock		9
κτάομαι	I acquire		7
κύκλῳ	(all) around	(*cycle*)	8
κῦμα, -ατος, τό	wave		5
κύων, -νός, ὁ	dog	(*cynic*)	5
λεπρός, -ά, -όν	leprous	(*leper*)	9
λέων, -οντος, ὁ	lion	(*lion*)	9
ληνός, -οῦ, ἡ	wine-press		5
λύκος, -ου, ὁ	wolf		6
μάγος, -ου, ὁ	Magus; magician	(*magic*)	6
μαίνομαι	I am mad	(cf. *man*ia)	5
μαργαρίτης, -ου, ὁ	pearl		9

μάταιος, -αία, -αιον	idle, useless		6
μεθύω	I am drunk	(*methyl* alcohol)	7
μέλας, -αινα, -αν	black	(*melan*choly)	6
μεστός, -ή, -όν	full		9
μιαίνω	I defile		5
μιμητής, -οῦ, ὁ	imitator	(cf. *mime*)	6
μνᾶ, μνάς, ἡ	mina		9
μόσχος, -ου, ὁ	calf		6
μῦθος, -ου, ὁ	tale, myth	(*myth*)	5
μυριάς, -άδος, ἡ	ten thousand, myriad	(*myriad*)	8

5.

νῆσος, -ου, ἡ	island		9
νήφω	I am sober, self-controlled		6
νότος, -ου, ὁ	south, south wind		7
ὀθόνιον, -ου, τό	linen cloth		5
οἰκτιρμός, -οῦ, ὁ	mercy		5
ὅπλον, -ου, τό	weapon		6
ὁρμάω	I set out, rush		5
ὅσιος, -ία, -ον	devout, holy		8
ὀσμή, -ῆς, ἡ	odor		6
ὀσφῦς, -ύος, ἡ	waist, loins		8
οὐρά, -ᾶς, ἡ	tail		5
παγίς, -ίδος, ἡ	trap		5
παίω	I strike, wound		5
παρακύπτω	I bend over		5
παροιμία, -ας, ἡ	proverb, figure		5
πενθερά, -ᾶς, ἡ	mother-in-law		6
πεποίθησις, -εως, ἡ	confidence		6
πηλός, -οῦ, ὁ	clay, mud		6
πήρα, -ας, ἡ	bag		6
πίναξ, -ακος, ἡ	dish		5
πιπράσκω	I sell		9
πλατεῖα, -ας, ἡ	street	(*place*)	9

πλευρά, -ᾶς, ἡ	side	(*pleur*isy)	5
πραιτώριον, -ου, τό	praetorium		8
πρέπω	I am fitting		7

6.

πταίω	I stumble		5
πτέρυξ, -υγος, ἡ	wing	(*pter*odactyl)	5
πωρόω	I harden		5
ῥίπτω	I throw down		7
ῥομφαία, -ας, ἡ	sword		7
σαπρός, -ά, -όν	rotten		8
σβέννυμι	I extinguish		8
σελήνη, -ης, ἡ	moon		9
σίδηρος, -ου, ὁ	iron		5
σπεῖρα, -ης, ἡ	cohort		7
σπήλαιον, -ου, τό	cave, den	(cf. *spel*unker)	6
σπυρίς, -ίδος, ἡ	basket		5
στάδιον, -ου, τό	stade	(*stadium*)	7
στάχυς, -υος, ὁ	head, ear (of grain)		5
στεῖρα, -ας, ἡ	barren	(cf. *ster*ile)	5
στενάζω	I sigh, groan		6
στῆθος, -ους, τό	chest, breast	(*stetho*scope)	5
στρωννύω	I spread		6
συμπνίγω	I crowd out, choke out		5
σύρω	I draw		5
τεῖχος, -ους, τό	(city) wall		9
τράχηλος, -ου, ὁ	neck, throat	(*trache*a)	7
τρόμος, -ου, ὁ	trembling	(*tremo*r)	5
τρώγω	I eat (audibly)		6

7.

ὑβρίζω	I treat arrogantly, insult	(cf. *hubris*)	5
ὑετός, -οῦ, ὁ	rain		5
ὑπερήφανος, -ον	arrogant, haughty		5
ὕπνος, -ου, ὁ	sleep	(*hypno*tism)	6
φαῦλος, -η, -ον	worthless, evil		6

φθάνω	I arrive; I precede		7
φθόνος, -ου, ὁ	envy		9
φλόξ, φλογός, ἡ	flame		7
φρέαρ, -ατος, τό	a well		7
φύλλον, -ου, τό	leaf	(chlorophyll)	6
φύραμα, -ατος, τό	dough		5
φυσιόω	I puff up, make proud		7
χαλκός, -οῦ, ὁ	brass, bronze, money		5
χάραγμα, -ατος, τό	mark, stamp	(cf. character)	8
κεῖλος, -ους, τό	lip		7
κειμών, -ῶνος, ὁ	winter, stormy weather		6
ὡσαννά	hosanna!		6

Part Five

Principal Parts of
Selected Important Verbs

An important part of learning the vocabulary of the Greek New Testament is learning the principal parts of numerous verbs. The student often learns these one by one in the daily lessons, but it is good to review them together. Some of the verbs presented below are irregular, and should be studied with special care. They have been chosen because they illustrate the different types of verbs, in addition to being words that occur fifty or more times in the New Testament. The verb forms in parentheses do not occur in the New Testament, but are given for illustrative reasons. Hyphenated forms are found only in compound verbs. The most basic meaning of the verb is given after the last principal part.

PRINCIPAL PARTS OF SELECTED IMPORTANT VERBS

Present	Future	Aorist	Perf. Act.	Perf. Mid.	Aorist Pass.	
ἀγαπάω	ἀγαπήσω	ἠγάπησα	ἠγάπηκα	ἠγάπημαι	ἠγαπήθην	love
ἄγω	ἄξω	ἤγαγον	(ἦχα)	-ἦγμαι	ἤχθην	lead
αἴρω	ἀρῶ	ἦρα	ἦρκα	ἦρμαι	ἤρθην	take up
ἀνοίγω	ἀνοίξω	ἠνέῳξα	ἀνέῳγα	ἀνέῳγμαι	ἀνεῴχθην	open
ἀποθνῄσκω	ἀποθαν- οῦμαι	ἀπέθανον	τέθνηκα			die
ἀποκτείνω	ἀποκτενῶ	ἀπέκτεινα	(ἀπέκτονα)			kill
ἀπόλλυμι	ἀπολέσω	ἀπώλεσα	ἀπόλωλα			destroy
ἀπολύω	ἀπολύσω	ἀπέλυσα	(ἀπολέλυκα)	ἀπολέλυμαι	ἀπελύθην	release
ἀποστέλλω	ἀποστελῶ	ἀπέστειλα	ἀπέσταλκα	ἀπέσταλμαι	ἀπεστάλην	send
ἀφίημι	ἀφήσω	ἀφῆκα	ἀφεῖκα	ἀφεῖμαι	ἀφέθην	forgive
βάλλω	βαλῶ	ἔβαλον	βέβληκα	βέβλημαι	ἐβλήθην	throw
γεννάω	γεννήσω	ἐγέννησα	γεγέννηκα	γεγέννημαι	ἐγεννήθην	beget
γίνομαι	γενήσομαι	ἐγενόμην	γέγονα	γεγέννημαι	ἐγενήθην	become
γράφω	γράψω	ἔγραψα	γέγραφα	γέγραμμαι	ἐγράφην	write
διδάσκω	διδάξω	ἐδίδαξα	(δεδίδαχα)	(δεδίδαγμαι)	ἐδιδάχθην	teach
δίδωμι	δώσω	ἔδοκα	δέδωκα	δέδομαι	ἐδόθην	give
ἐγείρω	ἐγερῶ	ἤγειρα	(ἐγήγερκα)	ἐγήγερμαι	ἠγέρθην	raise
ἔρχομαι	ἐλεύσομαι	ἦλθον	ἐλήλυθα			come
ἐσθίω	φάγομαι	ἔφαγον				eat
ἔχω	ἕξω	ἔσχον	ἔσχηκα	(ἔσχημαι)		have
ἵστημι	στήσω	ἔστησα	ἕστηκα	(ἕσταμαι)	ἐστάθην	stand
κηρύσσω	κηρύξω	ἐκήρυξα	(κεκήρυχα)	-κεκήρυγμαι	ἐκηρύχθην	preach
κρίνω	κρινῶ	ἔκρινα	κέκρικα	κέκριμαι	ἐκρίθην	judge
λαμβάνω	λήμψομαι	ἔλαβον	εἴληφα	εἴλημμαι	ἐλήφθην	take
λέγω	ἐρῶ	εἶπον	εἴρηκα	εἴρημαι	ἐρρέθην	say
ὁράω	ὄψομαι	εἶδον	ἑόρακα	(ἑώραμαι)	ὤφθην	see
πείθω	πείσω	ἔπεισα	πέποιθα	πέπεισμαι	ἐπείσθην	persuade, trust
πίνω	πίομαι	ἔπιον	πέπωκα	-πέπωμαι	-εποθην	drink
ποιέω	ποιήσω	ἐποίησα	πεποίηκα	πεποίημαι	(-εποιήθην)	do
σῴζω	σώσω	ἔσωσα	σέσωκα	σέσωσμαι	ἐσώθην	save
τίθημι	θήσω	ἔθηκα	τέθεικα	τέθειμαι	ἐτέθην	put
φέρω	οἴσω	ἤνεγκα	-ἐνήνοχα	(ἐνήνεγμαι)	ἠνέχθην	bring

Part Six

Numbers

The following numbers and related words from Parts Three and Four are brought together here for greater ease in memorization and review.

εἷς, μία, ἕν one

δύο two (*du*et)
δεύτερος, -α, -ον second (*Deutero*nomy)

τρεῖς, τρία three (cf. *tr*inity)
τρίς three times
τρίτος, -η, -ον third
τριάκοντα thirty

τέσσαρες four
τεσσαράκοντα forty
τέταρτος, -η, -ον fourth
τετρακισχίλιοι four thousand

εἰκοσιτέσσαρες twenty-four

_____

πέντε five (*pent*agon)
πεντήκοντα fifty
πεντακισχίλιοι five thousand

_____

ἕξ six
ἕκτος, -η, -ον sixth
ἑξήκοντα sixty

_____

ἑπτά seven
ἕβδομος, -η, -ον seventh

_____

ὀκτώ eight (*oct*opus)
ὄγδοὄς, -η, -ον eighth

_____

δέκα ten (*dec*ade)

_____

δώδεκα twelve

_____

δεκατέσσαρες fourteen

_____

χιλιάς, -άδος, ἡ (a group of) a thousand
χίλιοι, -αι, -α thousands

Index to Parts Three and Four

ἁμαρτωλός 24
ἀμήν 79
ἄμμος 86
ἄμπελος 60
ἀμπελών 60
ἀμφότεροι 82
ἄμωμος 86
ἄν 24
ἀνά 60
ἀναβλέπω 32
ἀναγγέλλω 23
ἀναγινώσκω 24
ἀναγκάζω 61
ἀναγκαῖος 61
ἀνάγκη 61
ἀνάγω 38
ἀνάθεμα 38
ἀναιρέω 61
ἀνάκειμαι 65
ἀνακλίνω 75
ἀνακράζω 43
ἀνακρίνω 35
ἀναλαμβάνω 27
ἀναμιμνήσκω 54
ἀνάπαυσις 69
ἀναπαύω 69
ἀναπέμπω 44
ἀναπίπτω 45
ἀναπληρόω 45
ἀνάστασις 33
ἀναστρέφω 51
ἀναστροφή 51
ἀνατέλλω 42
ἀνατολή 42
ἀναφέρω 47
ἀναχωρέω 61
ἀνέγκλητος 34
ἀνέχομαι 18
ἀνήρ 79
ἀνθίστημι 33
ἀνθρώπινος 16

ἄνθρωπος 16
ἀνθύπατος 86
ἀνίστημι 33
ἀνοίγω 39
ἀνομία 27
ἄνομος 27
ἀντί 82
ἀντίδικος 41
ἀντίκειμαι 65
ἀντιτάσσομαι 58
ἀντίχριστος 77
ἀνυπόκριτος 35
ἄνω 61
ἄνωθεν 60
ἄξιος 48
ἀξιόω 49
ἀξίως 49
ἀόρατος 20
ἀπαγγέλλω 23
ἀπάγω 38
ἅπαξ 61
ἀπαρνέομαι 49
ἀπαρχή 40
ἅπας 22
ἀπάτη 74
ἀπείθεια 28
ἀπειθέω 28
ἀπειθής 29
ἄπειμι 17
ἀπεκδέχομαι 40
ἀπέρχομαι 18
ἀπέχω 18
ἀπιστέω 28
ἀπιστία 28
ἄπιστος 28
ἁπλότης 86
ἀπό 78
ἀποδέχομαι 40
ἀποδημέω 86
ἀποδίδωμι 16
ἀποδοκιμάζω 25

ἀποθήκη 86
ἀποθνῄσκω 33
ἀποκαθίστημι 33
ἀποκαλύπτω 49
ἀποκάλυψις 49
ἀποκόπτω 63
ἀποκρίνομαι 35
ἀποκτείνω 80
ἀπολαμβάνω 27
ἀπολείπω 43
ἀπόλλυμι 39
ἀπολογέομαι 19
ἀπολογία 19
ἀπολύτρωσις 43
ἀπολύω 43
ἀπορέω 36
ἀποστέλλω 31
ἀποστερέω 86
ἀπόστολος 31
ἀποτάσσομαι 58
ἀποτίθημι 38
ἀποφέρω 47
ἅπτω 81
ἀπωθέομαι 86
ἀπώλεια 39
ἄρα 81
ἀργός 86
ἀργύριον 61
ἄργυρος 61
ἀρέσκω 61
ἀρεστός 61
ἀρετή 86
ἀριθμός 82
ἀρκέω 86
ἀρνέομαι 49
ἀρνίον 81
ἁρπάζω 62
ἅρπαξ 62
ἄρρωστος 86
ἄρσην 86
ἄρτι 81

98

δένδρον 83
δέομαι 32
δεξιός 40
δέρω 83
δέσμιος 50
δεσμός 50
δεσπότης 83
δεῦρο 62
δεῦτε 62
δεύτερος 32
δέχομαι 40
δέω 50
δή 42
δηλόω 87
δηνάριον 83
διά 78
διάβολος 31
διαθήκη 38
διακονέω 50
διακονία 50
διάκονος 50
διακρίνω 35
διαλέγομαι 19
διάλεκτος 19
διαλογίζομαι 19
διαλογισμός 19
διαμένω 35
διαμερίζω 54
διάνοια 54
διανοίγω 39
διαπεράω 69
διαρήσσω 74
διαρρήγνυμι 74
διασκορπίζω 74
διαστέλλομαι 31
διαστρέφω 51
διασῴζω 37
διατάσσω 58
διατίθημι 38
διατρίβω 74
διαφέρω 47

διαφθείρω 77
διαφθορά 77
διδασκαλία 41
διδάσκαλος 41
διδάσκω 41
διδαχή 41
δίδωμι 16
διεγείρω 32
διερμηνεύω 76
διέρχομαι 18
διηγέομαι 52
δίκαιος 41
δικαιοσύνη 41
δικαιόω 41
δικαίωμα 41
δικαίως 41
δίκτυον 83
διό 41
διότι 41
δίς 87
διψάω 83
διωγμός 50
διώκω 50
δόγμα 25
δοκέω 25
δοκιμή 25
δόκιμος 25
δοκός 87
δόλος 83
δόξα 25
δοξάζω 25
δουλεία 32
δουλεύω 32
δοῦλος 32
δουλόω 32
δράκων 83
δρέπανον 87
δύναμαι 25
δύναμις 25
δυνατός 25
δύο 32

δυσμή 51
δώδεκα 41
δῶμα 87
δωρεά 16
δωρεάν 16
δῶρον 16

ἐάν 17
ἑαυτοῦ 16
ἐάω 83
ἕβδομος 42
ἐγγίζω 50
ἐγγύς 50
ἐγείρω 32
ἐγκακέω 43
ἐγκαλέω 34
ἐγκαταλείπω 43
ἐγκεντρίζω 87
ἐγκόπτω 63
ἐγώ 17
ἔθνος 79
ἔθος 83
εἰ 17
εἰδωλόθυτος 28
εἰδωλολάτρης 28
εἴδωλον 28
εἰκῇ 87
εἰκοσιτέσσαρες 57
εἰκών 83
εἰμί 17
εἰς 17
εἰρήνη 80
εἷς 79
εἰσάγω 38
εἰσακούω 15
εἰσέρχομαι 18
εἴσοδος 35
εἰσπορεύομαι 36
εἰσφέρω 47
εἶτα 63
εἰρήνη 80

ἐπιλαμβάνομαι 27
ἐπιλανθάνομαι 75
ἐπιμένω 35
ἐπιπίπτω 45
ἐπιπλήσσω 70
ἐπισκιάζω 76
ἐπισκοπέω 64
ἐπιστολή 31
ἐπιστρέφω 51
ἐπισυνάγω 39
ἐπιταγή 58
ἐπιτάσσω 58
ἐπιτίθημι 38
ἐπιτελέω 57
ἐπιτιμάω 58
ἐπιτρέπω 64
ἐπιτυγχάνω 72
ἐπιφάνεια 58
ἐποικοδομέω 36
ἐπουράνιος 28
ἑπτά 42
ἐραυνάω 87
ἐργάζομαι 26
ἐργασία 26
ἐργάτης 26
ἔργον 26
ἐρημόομαι 52
ἔρημος 52
ἐριθεία 75
ἔρις 75
ἔρχομαι 18
ἐρωτάω 42
ἐσθής 87
ἐσθίω 27
ἔσχατος 80
ἔσω 17
ἔσωθεν 17
ἕτερος 80
ἔτι 80
ἑτοιμάζω 52
ἕτοιμος 52

εὖ 87
εὐαγγελίζομαι 23
εὐαγγέλιον 23
εὐάρεστος 61
εὐδοκέω 25
εὐδοκία 25
εὐθέως 42
εὐθύς 42
εὐκοπώτερος 67
εὐλογέω 19
εὐλογία 19
εὐλογητός 19
εὐπρόσδεκτος 40
εὑρίσκω 79
εὐσέβεια 64
εὐσχήμων 76
εὐφραίνω 59
εὐχαριστέω 29
εὐχαριστία 30
εὔχομαι 46
εὐώνυμος 28
ἐφάπαξ 61
ἐφίστημι 34
ἔχθρα 52
ἐχθρός 52
ἔχιδνα 87
ἔχω 18
ἕως 79

ζάω 32
ζῆλος 64
ζηλόω 64
ζηλωτής 64
ζημιόομαι 87
ζητέω 33
ζήτημα 33
ζήτησις 33
ζιζάνιον 87
ζόφος 87
ζυγός 87
ζύμη 64

ζωή 32
ζώνη 75
ζῷον 32
ζωοποιέω 22

ἤ 79
ἡγεμών 52
ἡγέομαι 52
ἤδη 42
ἥκω 81
ἡλικία 87
ἥλιος 81
ἡμέρα 27
ἡμέτερος 17
ἥμισυς 87
ἡσυχάζω 87

θάλασσα 80
θάνατος 33
θανατόω 33
θαρρέω 75
θαρσέω 75
θαυμάζω 52
θαυμαστός 52
θεάομαι 83
θέλημα 27
θέλω 27
θεμέλιον 64
θεμέλιος 64
θεμελιόω 64
θεός 78
θεραπεύω 81
θερίζω 65
θερισμός 65
θερμαίνομαι 88
θεωρέω 80
θηρίον 81
θησαυρίζω 65
θησαυρός 65
θλίβω 52
θλῖψις 52

κληρονομία 66
κληρονόμος 66
κλῆρος 66
κλῆσις 34
κλητός 34
κλίνη 75
κοιλία 83
κοιμάομαι 65
κοινός 66
κοινόω 66
κοινωνέω 66
κοινωνία 66
κοινωνός 66
κόκκινος 75
κόκκος 75
κολαφίζω 88
κολλάομαι 83
κόλπος 88
κονιορτός 88
κοπιάω 67
κόπος 67
κόπτω 63
κοράσιον 88
κοσμέω 27
κόσμος 27
κόφινος 88
κράβαττος 83
κράζω 43
κράσπεδον 88
κρατέω 53
κράτος 53
κραυγάζω 75
κραυγή 75
κρείττων 53
κρεμάννυμι 88
κρίμα 35
κρίνω 35
κρίσις 35
κριτής 35
κρούω 88
κρυπτός 67

κρύπτω 67
κτάομαι 88
κτίζω 67
κτίσις 67
κύκλῳ 88
κῦμα 88
κυριεύω 19
κύριος 19
κύων 88
κωλύω 84
κώμη 81
κωφός 84

λαλέω 27
λαμβάνω 27
λαμπάς 76
λαμπρός 76
λάμπω 76
λανθάνω 75
λαός 79
λατρεία 67
λατρεύω 67
λέγω 19
λείπω 43
λειτουργία 27
λειτουργός 27
λεπρός 88
λευκός 84
λέων 88
ληνός 88
λῃστής 84
λίαν 84
λιθάζω 43
λιθοβολέω 31
λίθος 43
λίμνη 84
λιμός 84
λογίζομαι 19
λόγος 19
λοιπός 43
λύκος 88

λυπέω 53
λύπη 53
λυχνία 67
λύχνος 67
λύω 43

μάγος 88
μαθητής 27
μαίνομαι 88
μακάριος 80
μακράν 67
μακρόθεν 67
μακροθυμέω 67
μακροθυμία 67
μακρός 67
μάλιστα 44
μᾶλλον 44
μανθάνω 27
μαργαρίτης 88
μαρτυρέω 44
μαρτυρία 44
μαρτύριον 44
μαρτύρομαι 44
μάρτυς 44
μαστιγόω 76
μάστιξ 76
μάταιος 89
μάχαιρα 81
μεγαλύνω 27
μέγας 27
μεθερμηνεύω 76
μεθίστημι 34
μεθύω 89
μέλας 89
μέλει 67
μέλλω 79
μέλος 81
μέν 27
μέντοι 27
μένω 35
μερίζω 54

μέριμνα 68
μεριμνάω 67
μερίς 54
μέρος 54
μεσίτης 44
μέσος 44
μεστός 89
μετά 20
μεταδίδωμι 16
μεταλαμβάνω 27
μεταμέλομαι 67
μετανοέω 54
μετάνοια 54
μεταξύ 20
μεταπέμπομαι 44
μετασχηματίζω 76
μετέχω 18
μέτοχος 18
μετρέω 68
μέτρον 68
μέτωπον 36
μέχρι 84
μή 20
μηδέ 20
μηδείς 20
μηκέτι 20
μήν 84
μήποτε 20
μήτε 20
μήτηρ 80
μήτι 20
μιαίνω 89
μικρός 81
μιμητής 89
μισέω 81
μισθός 81
μνᾶ 89
μνεία 54
μνῆμα 54
μνημεῖον 54
μνημονεύω 54

μοιχεύω 68
μοιχαλίς 68
μονογενής 16
μόνος 79
μόσχος 89
μῦθος 89
μυριάς 89
μύρον 84
μυστήριον 81
μωρία 68
μωρός 68

ναί 81
νεανίσκος 68
νεκρός 79
νέος 68
νεφέλη 84
νήπιος 84
νῆσος 89
νηστεία 68
νηστεύω 68
νήφω 89
νικάω 82
νίπρω 84
νοέω 54
νόημα 54
νομίζω 27
νομικός 27
νόμος 27
νόσος 84
νότος 89
νουθετέω 54
νοῦς 54
νύμφη 68
νυμφίος 68
νῦν 35
νυνί 35
νύξ 80

ξενίζω 68
ξένος 68

ξηραίνω 68
ξηρός 68
ξύλον 84

ὁ, ἡ, τό 20
ὄγδοος 76
ὅδε 20
ὁδηγέω 39
ὁδηγός 39
ὁδός 35
ὀδούς 84
ὅθεν 21
ὀθόνιον 89
οἶδα 28
οἰκέω 36
οἰκία 36
οἰκοδεσπότης 36
οἰκοδομή 36
οἰκονομέω 36
οἰκονομία 36
οἰκονόμος 36
οἶκος 35
οἰκουμένη 36
οἰκτιρμός 89
οἶνος 82
οἷος 21
ὀκτώ 76
ὀλίγος 82
ὅλος 79
ὀμνύω 82
ὁμοθυμαδόν 51
ὅμοιος 54
ὁμοιόω 54
ὁμοίωμα 54
ὁμοίως 54
ὁμολογέω 19
ὁμολογία 20
ὀνειδίζω 76
ὀνειδισμός 76
ὄνομα 28
ὀνομάζω 28

ὄντως 17
ὄξος 76
ὀξύς 76
ὄπισθεν 54
ὀπίσω 54
ὅπλον 89
ὁποῖος 37
ὅπως 37
ὅραμα 20
ὁράω 20
ὀργή 55
ὀργίζομαι 55
ὁρίζω 69
ὅριον 69
ὅρκος 84
ὁρμάω 89
ὄρος 80
ὅς 21
ὅσιος 89
ὀσμή 89
ὅσος 21
ὅστις 21
ὀσφῦς 89
ὅταν 24
ὅτε 21
ὅτι 21
οὗ 21
οὐ 21
οὐαί 82
οὐδέ 21
οὐδείς 21
οὐδέποτε 21
οὐκέτι 21
οὖν 78
οὔπω 21
οὐρά 89
οὐράνιος 28
οὐρανός 28
οὖς 82
οὔτε 21
οὗτος 21

οὕτως 21
οὐχί 21
ὀφειλέτης 55
ὀφείλω 55
ὀφθαλμός 36
ὄφις 84
ὄχλος 79

παγίς 89
πάθημα 55
παιδεία 44
παιδεύω 44
παιδίον 44
παιδίσκη 44
παῖς 44
παίω 89
πάλαι 69
παλαιός 69
πάλιν 79
πᾶς 21
πανουργία 27
πανταχοῦ 22
παντοκράτωρ 22
πάντοτε 29
πάντως 22
παρά 79
παραβολή 31
παραγγελία 23
παραγγέλλω 23
παραγίνομαι 16
παράγω 39
παραδέχομαι 40
παραδίδωμι 16
παράδοσις 16
παραιτέομαι 39
παρακαλέω 34
παράκλησις 34
παράκλητος 34
παρακύπτω 89
παραλαμβάνω 27
παραλύομαι 44

παραλυτικός 44
παραπορεύομαι 36
παράπτωμα 45
παρασκευή 71
παρατηρέω 47
παρατίθημι 38
παραχρῆμα 60
πάρειμι 17
παρεμβολή 31
παρέρχομαι 18
παρέχω 18
παρθένος 84
παρίστημι 34
παροιμία 89
παρουσία 17
παρρησία 46
παρρησιάζομαι 46
πάσχω 55
πατάσσω 84
πατέω 45
πατήρ 21
πατρίς 21
παύω 69
πείθω 28
πεινάω 84
πειράζω 55
πειρασμός 55
πέμπω 45
πενθερά 89
πενθέω 69
πένθος 69
πεντακισχίλιοι 55
πέντε 55
πεντήκοντα 55
πεποίθησις 89
πέραν 69
περιάγω 39
περιβλέπομαι 32
περιζώννυμι 75
περίκειμαι 65
περίλυπος 53

προσφωνέω 38
πρόσωπον 36
πρότερος 56
πρόφασις 36
προφητεία 36
προφητεύω 36
προφήτης 36
πρωΐ 85
πρωτοκλισία 75
πρῶτος 79
πρωτότοκος 47
πταίω 90
πτέρυξ 90
πτῶμα 45
πτωχός 82
πύλη 70
πυλών 70
πυνθάνομαι 85
πῦρ 46
πυρετός 46
πυρόομαι 46
πωλέω 85
πῶλος 85
πώποτε 37
πωρόω 90
πώς 37
πῶς 37

ῥαββί 85
ῥάβδος 85
ῥήγνυμι 74
ῥῆμα 46
ῥίζα 85
ῥίπτω 90
ῥομφαία 90
ῥύομαι 85

σάββατον 80
σαλεύω 85
σάλπιγξ 70
σαλπίζω 70

σαπρός 90
σαρκικός 37
σάρξ 37
σβέννυμι 90
σεαυτοῦ 22
σέβομαι 64
σεισμός 70
σείω 70
σελήνη 90
σημαίνω 46
σημεῖον 46
σήμερον 27
σιγάω 85
σίδηρος 90
σῖτος 85
σιωπάω 85
σκανδαλίζω 56
σκάνδαλον 56
σκεῦος 71
σκηνή 71
σκηνόω 71
σκιά 76
σκληρός 77
σκληρύνω 77
σκοπέω 64
σκορπίος 74
σκοτία 56
σκοτίζομαι 56
σκότος 56
σός 22
σοφία 47
σοφός 47
σπεῖρα 90
σπείρω 47
σπέρμα 47
σπεύδω 71
σπήλαιον 90
σπλαγχνίζομαι 71
σπλάγχνον 71
σπόρος 47
σπουδάζω 71

σπουδή 71
σπυρίς 90
στάδιον 90
στάσις 34
σταυρός 57
σταυρόω 57
στάχυς 90
στεῖρα 90
στενάζω 90
στέφανος 85
στῆθος 90
στήκω 34
στηρίζω 85
στοιχεῖον 77
στοιχέω 77
στολή 31
στόμα 80
στράτευμα 57
στρατεύομαι 57
στρατηγός 57
στρατιώτης 57
στρέφω 51
στρωννύω 90
σύ 22
συγγενής 16
συγκαλέω 34
συγχαίρω 30
συζητέω 33
συλλαλέω 27
συλλαμβάνω 27
συλλέγω 20
συμβάλλω 31
συμβούλιον 49
συμπνίγω 90
συμφέρω 48
συμφωνέω 38
σύν 79
συνάγω 39
συναγωγή 39
συνανάκειμαι 65
σύνδουλος 32

φανερόω 58
φαῦλος 90
φείδομαι 85
φέρω 47
φεύγω 58
φημί 37
φθάνω 91
φθαρτός 77
φθείρω 77
φθόνος 91
φθορά 77
φιάλη 85
φιλαδελφία 59
φιλέω 58
φίλημα 59
φίλος 58
φλόξ 91
φοβέομαι 48
φόβος 48
φονεύς 72
φονεύω 72
φόνος 72
φορέω 48
φόρος 48
φορτίον 48
φρέαρ 91
φρονέω 59
φρόνιμος 59
φυλακή 59
φυλάσσω 59
φυλή 59
φύλλον 91
φύραμα 91
φυσιόω 91

φύσις 59
φυτεύω 59
φωνέω 38
φωνή 38
φῶς 48
φωτεινός 48
φωτίζω 48

χαίρω 29
χαλκός 91
χαρά 29
χάραγμα 91
χαρίζομαι 29
χάρις 29
χάρισμα 29
χεῖλος 91
χειμών 91
χείρ 79
χειροποίητος 22
χείρων 85
χήρα 82
χιλίαρχος 39
χιλιάς 73
χίλιοι 73
χιτών 85
χορός 85
χορτάζω 73
χόρτος 73
χράομαι 59
χρεία 59
χρῄζω 59
χρῆμα 59
χρηματίζω 59
χρηστός 59

χρηστότης 60
χρίω 77
χρονίζω 60
χρόνος 60
χρυσίον 73
χρυσός 73
χρυσοῦς 73
χωλός 85
χώρα 60
χωρέω 60
χωρίζω 60
χωρίον 60
χωρίς 60

ψάλλω 77
ψαλμός 77
ψεύδομαι 73
ψευδομαρτυρέω 44
ψεῦδος 73
ψευδοπροφήτης 73
ψεύστης 73
ψυχή 38
ψυχικός 38
ὦ 85
ὧδε 20
ᾠδή 77
ὥρα 80
ὡς 23
ὡσαννά 91
ὡσαύτως 23
ὡσεί 23
ὥσπερ 23
ὥστε 23
ὠφελέω 85